RONALD REAGAN

RONALD REAGAN

His Life Story
in Pictures

STANLEY P. FRIEDMAN

DODD, MEAD & COMPANY   New York

Published by Dodd, Mead & Company, Inc.
79 Madison Avenue, New York, N.Y. 10016
Distributed in Canada by
McClelland and Stewart Limited, Toronto
Manufactured in the United States of America
Designed by Stanley S. Drate, Folio Graphics Co., Inc.
A James A. Bryans Book
First Edition

1 2 3 4 5 6 7 8 9 10

Library of Congress Cataloging-in-Publication Data

Friedman, Stanley P., 1925–
   Ronald Reagan, his life story in pictures.

   1. Reagan, Ronald—Pictorial works.   2. Presidents—
United States—Pictorial works.   I. Title.
E877.2.F74   1986   973.927′092′4 [B]   86-11530
ISBN 0-396-08827-9 (pbk.)

Contents

1 Growing Up (1911–1927) 7

2 College (1928–1932) 17

3 Radio to the Movies (1933–1938) 25

4 Life in Hollywood (1939–1940) 35

5 Starring Ronald Reagan: A Movie Album 45

6 The Middle Years: Marriage, War, Divorce, Screen Actors Guild (1940–1948) 60

7 Nancy (1949) 66

8 From "GE Theatre" Host to Governor (1950–1966) 76

9 Governor of California and Candidate for the Presidency (1968–1978) 86

10 The Race for the Presidency (1979–1980) 96

11 The Assassination Attempt (1981) 108

12 China and Ireland (1984) 115

13 Campaign and Reelection (1984) 123

14 The Cancer Crisis (1985) 132

15 Reagan at the Summit/The Gander and *Challenger* Tragedies (1985–1986) 143

Selected Bibliography 159

Contents

1
GROWING UP
(1911–1927)

The story of Ronald Wilson Reagan and his family is the story of small-town America and the pursuit of the American dream. It is the story of two generations struggling through the hard times of the early decades of our century and the terrible Great Depression of the 1930s. Although Jack Reagan, the dreamer, and Nelle Reagan, the doer and unsinkable optimist, never caught up with their dream, they never stopped trying. And they gave to their sons, Neil and Ronald, a priceless heritage: a belief in the "old-fashioned values"—a conviction that self-reliance and honorable hard work can bring the good life within reach of everyone.

"I suppose we were poor," Ronald Reagan has often said, "but we never knew we were poor." This was the legacy of Jack and Nelle. When things hit bottom and the Reagans were living in one room and cooking over a hot plate, with Jack unemployed and Nelle working as a seamstress, the boys believed this was just a temporary setback.

"He was the most American of Americans—an embodiment of the Declaration of Independence—the Fourth of July incarnate," wrote historian James Parton of Andrew Jackson. It is equally a description of President Ronald Wilson Reagan. And to discover the forces that shaped the man, one must go back to his boyhood days in the small towns of Illinois.

Ronald Reagan did not come easily into this world on February 6, 1911. At that time the family lived in a small three-room apartment over a general store in Tampico, Illinois. It was a time when babies were usually born at home, rarely in a hospital, and Nelle Wilson Reagan had hired a midwife to help her give birth.

The midwife saw complications ahead, but Tampico, a town of less than a thousand, did not have a doctor. Fortunately, the midwife found Dr. Harry Terry stranded overnight in a boarding house by a winter blizzard. He delivered Ronald Wilson Reagan, but he warned Nelle Reagan never to give birth again. To his father, Ronald looked like a fat little Dutchman, and so the chubby, sweet-natured infant was nicknamed Dutch.

Jack Reagan lost and left jobs frequently; he was an alcoholic. He would go for months at a time without taking a drink and then suddenly disappear on a bender for a week or two while the family waited patiently for his return. Sober, he would travel around looking for work, primarily as a shoe salesman, moving his family to a new town for a fresh start with each new job.

Though Jack had weaknesses, he also had a great strength— he worked very hard when he was sober. He never stopped aiming for success, convinced that one day he would become prosperous as the proprietor of his own store. Jack Reagan believed wholeheartedly in the American dream. If a person worked hard enough, he told young Ronald, there was no world he could not conquer.

Nelle Wilson Reagan, a small auburn-haired woman with bright blue eyes, was the strong one in the family. Of sturdy Scotch-Irish stock, she was a religious woman and spent a great part of her life doing charitable work. (Ronald Reagan has called her "a practical do-gooder.") She was a cheerful, optimistic woman and urged both of her boys to persist, to always give their best to each endeavor.

The plump, one-year-old Ronald Reagan in 1912 (right) and his brother, Neil, three. Neil had hoped for a sister and wasn't sure he liked the male competition.

UPI/BETTMANN

Family portrait, circa 1915. Neil (left) and Ronald stand on a table for better visibility. Jack and Nelle Reagan sometimes suffered from small-town attitudes toward what was then called a "mixed marriage." (Jack was Catholic and Nelle was Protestant.)

During those early years, the Reagans fought a continual battle with poverty. When Jack worked for Marshall Field, they lived in a small, chilly three-room flat in South Chicago. It was illuminated by gaslight—if and when they had a quarter to drop in the meter down the hall.

On Saturday afternoon, Neil (two years older than Dutch and nicknamed Moon after the character in the comic strip "Moon Mullins") was sent regularly by his mother across the street to the butcher shop, with a dime to buy a soupbone. Nelle instructed Moon also to ask the butcher for a free liver for their cat. (They didn't have one.) In those days liver was routinely discarded by the butcher, so Moon's request was usually granted. The liver was Sunday dinner; the bone was for making a big pot of soup, which was kept on the stove for the whole week. Nelle would stretch the soup, adding water, carrots, and potatoes, to make it last until the next Saturday.

When Ronald Reagan was nine, his family finally managed to put down roots. They moved to Dixon, Illinois, a town one hundred-odd miles due west of Chicago. ("Dixon is my home town," Ronald Reagan says today.) Dutch went through his last three years of elementary school and all of his high school years in Dixon and called it home while he was away at college for four years.

Jack Reagan and his family were a rarity in Dixon. They were the only Democrats in town, and Jack was a liberal by the standards of that time and place. Furthermore, Jack and his older son, Moon, were Catholics in a town devoted to Protestant morals and Republican politics. Nelle and the younger son, Ronald, were Protestants, members of the Church of Christ. Nelle, a Protestant, had married Jack in his Roman Catholic church, agreeing to the stipulation that their children be raised as Catholics. The family split came about when Jack stopped attending services after the birth of Neil. Nelle subsequently felt it proper to take young Ronald to her church.

It was Nelle who first exposed Ronald to dramatics. After dinner the family regularly gathered in the living room and she recited dramatic passages in impassioned tones. Ronald was chosen to perform in Sunday School plays, but he was shy and resented giving up his time outdoors to take part in rehearsals.

Nelle Reagan, with only an elementary school education, was determined that her boys would be well prepared for school and college, and she read extensively to them in their preschool years. Little Dutch, even then a "quick study," was reading

Tampico, Illinois: A 1917 class photo of Ronald and thirty schoolmates on the front steps of their one-room schoolhouse. Ronald, nicknamed Dutch, is in the second row on the end, hand to mouth. A first-grader here, he never made it to the next grade in Tampico, as the hard-up Reagan family made one of its frequent moves shortly after this picture was taken.

He played no instrument, but, at nine in 1920, Ronald Reagan could lead a band. He became a baton boy when he joined the Dixon, Illinois, YMCA. The "Y" also taught him to swim, a skill that would serve him in good stead in the years to come.

Dutch Reagan, age twelve, in 1923, wearing knickers, his sleeves rolled up, sporting a Sunday tie. He may have been about to take off the tie and join his chums for a game of football, which was becoming his number one passion.

fluently, to the pride of his parents, well before he entered first grade.

What no one knew for twelve years was that Ronald was extremely nearsighted. He assumed that everyone saw the world as he did, with distant objects a mere blur. At school, he made sure he sat in the front row. Because he had (and retains) a photographic memory, he was able to cope with his undiagnosed handicap.

Then one day while out riding in the family car, twelve-year-old Ronald realized that brother Moon was reading road signs that he could not make out. He reached for his mother's glasses on the dashboard and put them on.

"When I picked up my mother's glasses," Reagan writes in his autobiography, *Where's the Rest of Me?*, "the miracle of seeing was beyond believing. I was astounded to find out the trees had sharply defined separate leaves, houses had a definite texture, and the hills really made a clear silhouette against the sky."

Shortly before the discovery of his nearsightedness, Dutch Reagan discovered sports. A well-to-do boy in the next block bought the very first football in the town of Dixon, and all the boys in the neighborhood came to play the game.

Dutch loved the wild charge down the field and the pileup. But when he ended up under the pile, he began to feel a certain panic in the darkness under the heap of bodies. He thought about giving up the game, but he couldn't—the love of competition kept pulling him back. He remembered his mother's admonition not to give up, to keep trying at all cost. It was advice that would come back to him many times in his life.

A 1928 yearbook photo of young Reagan, wearing his favorite costume, a football jersey and shoulder pads. Popular with boys and girls, he was a school leader and football star at Dixon Northside High School, unaware of disappointments that lay ahead at college.

Dixon was a small town of less than ten thousand inhabitants, but to Ronald it seemed as varied and fascinating as the largest city. On Saturdays he went to the movies to see Tom Mix and William S. Hart. These celluloid cowboys became his earliest heroes, a part of his life forever.

Ronald spent hours in the afternoon reading adventure books in the library. He was active in many outdoor pursuits, but it was football that was the center of his life; he practiced all summer for the fall football season.

Upon graduating from grammar school, Dutch Reagan, then thirteen, went to Dixon High on the Northside. Moon was already attending Dixon High School on the Southside and had become a star football player there. Dutch ached to play competitive sports like his big brother. In football, because of his poor eyesight, he couldn't play in the backfield, catch a pass, or make a tackle in the open field. But he found he could play on the line, where he was face-to-face with his opponent.

In his first year he didn't even make the scrub team—he was too small at five-three and 108 pounds. But Dutch didn't give up. No matter how disappointed he felt sitting on the bench, he never missed a practice session. He had his dream and he was determined to make it come true.

At last, in his third year, he got his break. The team's right guard reported in sick the day of the game. "Reagan," shouted the coach in the locker room just before the game, "you're starting at right guard." Dutch Reagan was slow in the game action, but he played ferociously and more than held his own with the fellows on the other side of the line. The coach couldn't deny his enthusiasm, grit, and stick-to-itiveness. He'd never had a kid try harder for him. From that day forward, through his junior and senior years, Dutch Reagan had a permanent starting slot.

Reagan shot up in his senior year to his present six feet one inch; he gained thirty pounds, weighing in at 165. A remarkable change came over the youth now that he was a first-string player. He blossomed, becoming sociable and outgoing, one of the most popular kids in school with both boys and girls.

He joined the drama society and played the lead in Phillip Barry's *You and I*. Now he found dramatics fun and exciting; he understood at last why his mother so loved to see all the plays put on in Dixon. It was the springtime of his life, and possibilities were opening up everywhere.

"Life is just one sweet song, so let the music begin," he said in his senior yearbook. The "music" young Reagan had in mind was college and, of course, football. But he had to earn his own way; obviously Jack and Nelle Reagan had no money to help him through school.

A foretaste of stardom. The play You and I, *with Ronald Reagan in a leading role, was staged at Dixon High in his junior year (1927). Top, he is seated beside the popular Margaret "Mugs" Cleaver. Bottom, he's kneeling, strumming a guitar, facing Mugs. Later, she would play a fateful role in the real-life drama of young Ronald Reagan.*

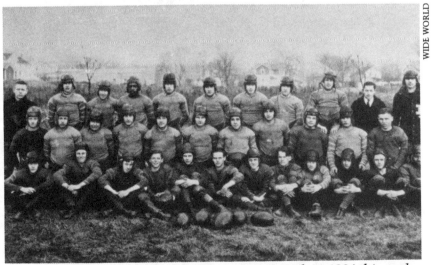

Dutch Reagan, the ardent footballer, at Dixon High in 1926, his sophomore year. He is in the front row, fourth from the left. He was still warming the bench, dreaming of great moments to come. His brother Neil, nicknamed Moon, was already a star at Dixon Southside High.

Dutch, wide-shouldered and handsome in his lifeguard suit, in a photo taken at Lowell Park in 1927. The rushing waters of Rock River sometimes made the beach dangerous. Dutch Reagan's rescues were frequent but not always appreciated.

Donald (sic) Reagan pictured in Dixonia, *the high school yearbook, 1928. His theme in the yearbook didn't anticipate the bumps and jolts he'd experience along the road of adult life.*

A menacing Dutch Reagan playing a villain in the drama Captain Applejack. *He is fifth from the left, in a hostile stance. It was his senior year in high school (1928). He liked the stage because, as he said, it enabled him "to show off," but it was far down his list of interests.*

The president, First Lady, and Neil Reagan standing in front of Ronald Reagan's boyhood home in Dixon, at a dedication ceremony making it a national shrine, funded by public donations. Ronald lived nine years in Dixon, in six separate houses. The peripatetic Reagans lived in this house from 1920 to 1924, during which time the future president went from fifth grade through his freshman year in high school.

Despite the sign, many places can lay claim to being Reagan's home in his "formative years."

BOYHOOD HOME OF
PRESIDENT
Ronald Wilson Reagan
HIS FORMATIVE YEARS

15

In the summer of 1926 he got a job at a local construction site for thirty-five cents an hour, digging foundations. It was tough, boring labor, but it put muscles on his lean frame, and he earned two hundred dollars, which he put in the bank for his college fund.

In 1927 he got a job as a lifeguard at Lowell Park; it paid fifteen dollars a week. He went on duty at eight in the morning and worked until sundown, sometimes later.

Ronald Reagan learned a great deal about people in that job. Over a period of seven summers, he rescued seventy-five men, women, and children. Most people, he found, hated being saved in public, but he did receive one memorable reward—an old man gave him ten dollars for rescuing his upper plate.

By the time he graduated from Dixon Northside High School and was ready to go to college, young Dutch had found a partner. He and Margaret "Mugs" Cleaver, a sparkling brunette, daughter of a Dixon minister, were in love and planned to go off to Eureka College together.

Ronald Reagan had four hundred dollars saved up to get him through the first year.

Tampico, Illinois. This building, now a bank, contains the upstairs apartment where Ronald Reagan was born on a snowy February day in 1911.

UPI/BETTMANN

2
COLLEGE
(1928–1932)

From the age of fourteen, Ronald Reagan had wanted to go to Eureka College, a small private school 120 miles south of Dixon near Peoria. He wanted to emulate his hero, Garland Waggoner, son of a Dixon minister, who had played four brilliant years of football there. For years Dutch had kept news stories of Waggoner's wonderful exploits.

Dutch Reagan and Margaret Cleaver arrived at Eureka in the fall of 1928, and Reagan fell in love at once with the school and its red brick Georgian buildings. He had found a second home.

The Depression came to the Midwest in 1928, a year ahead of the famous 1929 Wall Street crash. Low on funds, Ronald got a job washing dishes at the "Teke" house (the Tau Kappa Epsilon fraternity, which he had pledged) in exchange for his room and won a sports scholarship to pay for half of his tuition. Later, in his junior and senior years, he earned his way as the school's swim coach and pool lifeguard.

Ronald Reagan never played in a single football game during his first year at Eureka. He sat on the bench. He believed for a while that Coach McKinzie was prejudiced against him, rationalizing away the hard truth that he simply wasn't good enough to make the team.

But other skills began to emerge, and Reagan received his baptism in politics as a freshman at Eureka. He discovered he could successfully exhort the student crowd to act, to follow his lead, and he liked it.

Eureka's new president, Bert Wilson, had devised a plan to save the perpetually broke school from running a constant deficit by cutting faculty and certain courses, including some that

Dutch Reagan, budding thespian (top row, third from left), photographed in 1930 with fellow members of the Eureka College dramatic fraternity, Alpha Epsilon Sigma. This is one of the few pictures ever taken of Reagan wearing glasses.

juniors and seniors needed to graduate. The cuts would leave part of the graduating class without a degree and damage the school's academic standing. Encouraged by the faculty, the students planned a strike. They would refuse to attend classes if the cuts went through.

On Friday night just before fall vacation, President Wilson and the trustees held a meeting to vote on the budget and cuts. The students, some in night clothes, gathered in the chapel from all over the campus for a mass midnight meeting to protest the plan.

Ronald was a strike leader among the freshmen. Because he had no vested interest in the changes, the students, including upperclassmen, chose him to present a strike motion. He rose and gave a long, impassioned speech, and when he finally presented the motion the students rose to their feet shouting and voted to strike. Faculty members joined them. As Ronald Reagan tells it in his autobiography, "It was heady wine. Hell, with two more lines I could've had them riding through every Middlesex village and farm—without horses yet."

At home that summer, still sulking over Coach McKinzie's imagined prejudice, Ronald decided he would not go back to school for his sophomore year. He had only two hundred dollars in the bank after his summer lifeguard job, and even with a scholarship he would have but half the tuition.

He said a sad good-bye to Mugs Cleaver the night before she was to leave for her second year at Eureka. He was staying in Dixon, where he had a winter job working with a surveying crew.

The next morning he looked outside and saw rain. It was a depressing no-work day. Sitting on the edge of the bed, he felt a

Ronald (top left) plays a lead part, a shepherd who dies, in Edna St. Vincent Millay's one-act pacifist play Aria da Capo, *performed by the Eureka College players in a national competition in which they won a coveted second place. Ronald was cited for an outstanding performance. Seated (front, left) is "Mugs" Cleaver, to whom Reagan became engaged on graduation.*

sudden impulse to call Mugs. He wanted to go with her to Eureka in her father's car.

By the time Dutch and Mugs arrived on campus, the rain had stopped. The fall air was clear and the sky was a brilliant blue. It was perfect day for a big football game; he could feel it in the air.

He visited Coach McKinzie. The coach showed him the new football uniforms and that clinched it—he had to stay. He told McKinzie his financial troubles. McKinzie called the school's financial administrator, who agreed to defer Reagan's tuition— he could repay the school after he graduated and found work. They also found him a paying job washing dishes and waiting tables at Lyda Woods, the girls' dorm.

He called home to give Nelle the good news—he was staying in school. Nelle said she, too, had good news. Moon no longer thought college was a joke.

Moon had been working in a cement factory for two years. Ronald, wanting his brother to be someone important in life, not just a factory worker, had tried to persuade him to go to college, but Neil simply did not want to hear it from his kid brother.

Ronald saw an opportunity to be a hero—to work out a plan and spring it on Moon dramatically. First he got Moon his old job washing dishes at the Teke fraternity house. Teke also promised to pledge Neil, so Moon had a place to live and eat. Then Ronald went to Coach McKinzie and McKinzie offered Moon a scholarship. Like Ronald, he would not have to pay any tuition until after he graduated.

Neil turned it all down. Nelle laced into him for being foolish. That did it. Neil hitched a ride to Eureka and signed up for classes. His rise in later years, becoming a vice-president at McCann-Erickson, the giant international advertising agency, is due in some part to Ronald's help in getting him into college. Today the Reagan Sports Center at Eureka is named after both Ron and Neil.

Now that they were in college together, Ronald at last found an opportunity as an upperclassman to square up all the times he'd been badgered and teased by his big brother. At the frat house, Ronald whacked freshman Moon's bottom with a wooden paddle, with whopping, energetic swings that Moon claims he can feel to this very day.

Dutch Reagan had yet to make first-string football. Then came a break. Teke house had pledged Enos Cole, a transfer who had played on the famous Northwestern College team and then as a senior had become Eureka's quarterback. The two fraternity brothers and sports addicts became close friends.

One day during scrimmage, Cole was sidelined by an old knee injury. Ronald was playing right end on the second team on defense. Cole began whispering anticipated plays to Ronald. Four times Dutch had the jump on his foes' strategy. He sidestepped the opposition and stopped the plays cold.

McKinzie told Ron to keep it up, he was doing fine. That inspired Ronald. Two weeks later he showed McKinzie again that he had the right stuff. He got promoted to the first team. After that he played in every game for the next three years.

Reagan as a sophomore (top row, far left) with his class, in 1930. It was in his second year, he has said, that he began to feel a deep attachment to Eureka, one that has never left him.

EUREKA COLLEGE

Fraternity man Dutch Reagan (third from left, front row, wearing bow tie) in 1930 with fellow members gathered on the steps of Tau Kappa Epsilon House.

Dutch Reagan was Eureka's Mr. Everything in swimming, serving as swim team coach and earning his room and board as pool lifeguard. He did well as an intercollegiate competitor.

Right guard Ronald Reagan (first row, second from right) in his junior year, wearing the lightly padded football uniform that was typical of the day.

Football at Eureka was Reagan's consuming passion, but for a long time it was an unrequited love.

Ronald Wilson Reagan's senior yearbook picture (1932). He was getting respectable grades, relying more on his phenomenal memory than on "hitting the books."

By the time he was ready to graduate in 1932, he was a big man on campus. His sports reputation was that of a plugger, a guy who never gave up. Like his mother, he had the optimist's knack for raising people's spirits, for taking the high road. An articulate young man with an opinion on everything, he was also envied because he did well with very little studying. The night before an exam, he'd thumb through the text for an hour then, using his photographic memory to good advantage, he would write a satisfactory paper the next day. Not really interested in intellectual pursuits, he majored in sports and student activities.

Dutch Reagan served three years as president of the Booster Club, three years as a first-string guard on the football team, and three years as the principal basketball cheerleader. He was the school's number one swimmer for three years and spent two years as swimming coach. He was feature editor of the yearbook and a member of the student senate for two years, serving as president for one year.

Most important, he was active in the drama society. In Edna St. Vincent Millay's *Aria da Capo*, Ronald played a shepherd who dies a moving, dramatic death. The drama society entered

Ronald Reagan returns to Eureka College in 1955 to help celebrate the school's 100th anniversary. He'd washed dishes his first two years in school to pay for his board, but, he noted, it was more fun later when he worked in Lyda Woods, the girls' dormitory.

the one-act play in the Eva Le Gallienne Competition at Northwestern, going up against the drama departments of Harvard and Yale, among others. *Aria da Capo* took a coveted second place, and Ronald Reagan earned an honorable mention for his acting.

In their senior year at Eureka College, Ronald gave Margaret an engagement ring. Everybody expected them to marry. At graduation ceremonies in June of 1932, the seniors passed the school president in pairs, carrying strands of ivy between them. The president cut the linking ivy to symbolize their parting from college. However, when Ron and Mugs passed in review on the podium, the president smiled knowingly and did not cut the ivy that bound them.

"Everything good that has happened to me—everything—started here on this campus. . . ." said Ronald Reagan on an alumni visit to Eureka years later. One newsman reported that the happiest time of Ronald Wilson Reagan's 1980 presidential campaign was the evening he came home to Eureka College to shouts of "Dutch!" and "We want Reagan!" as the star graduate of the class of '32. It was an emotional moment worthy of a scene from one of his own movies.

At Eureka he had tested and affirmed the advice and beliefs he had received from his parents. He had begun to make his own American dream come true.

3
RADIO TO THE MOVIES (1933–1938)

*I*n 1932 the American dream was crumbling; there were no jobs to be had. Ronald Wilson Reagan graduated from Eureka College and joined the Depression millions out of work.

Neil's old cement plant had closed down. Jack Reagan's dream of at last running his own shop had also died—Jack's Fashion Boot Shop, the store he had opened with a partner, was bankrupt.

Nelle brought in the family's only money for a time, fourteen dollars a week, working as a seamstress in the back room of a Dixon dress shop.

Jack sublet their house. He used part of the money to pay rent on a three-room apartment that he, Nelle, and Ron moved into. Ron slept on the couch. Nelle cooked on a hot plate. A neighbor heated their oven food and handed the hot meals to them through a window.

That summer Ronald was back as a lifeguard at Lowell Park, where he met a wealthy businessman, Sid Altschuler. Altschuler, a Kansas City native, had married a woman from Dixon; Ron taught their two daughters to swim.

Sid asked Ron a simple question: What kind of job would it take to make him happy in life? Radio announcing, the young lifeguard answered without second thought. It was a dream spoken aloud for the first time.

Altschuler thought it an excellent choice. Radio had a big, growing future. He told Ron to go to Chicago because it was the radio center of the Midwest and advised him to apply at every station and take any job just to get a foot in the door. And don't quit, Altschuler counseled. Keep plugging away. Keep going back if they refuse you.

Ronald Reagan's first radio broadcasting job in Davenport, Iowa. Station WOC was owned by Colonel B. J. Palmer of the Palmer School of Chiropractic; the call letters WOC stood for World of Chiropractic. A boyhood stunt stood Ronald in good stead here.

Inspired, Ron hitchhiked to Chicago after the park closed in September and stayed with a fraternity brother. The big city awed him, but he was determined to get into radio.

Filled with hope and optimism, he made the rounds of every studio. He never once made it past the station manager's secretary for a tryout, and he ended his first few job-hunting days discouraged and confused.

A secretary at NBC finally took pity on the good-looking young man after his third visit. Go to the sticks and get a job first, she told him. When you have experience try us again.

Meanwhile he and Mugs were drifting apart. While on vacation in Europe, Mugs met a handsome attorney in the foreign service. They fell in love and the attorney proposed. Dutch received a "Dear John" letter and with it one engagement ring. For months afterward it was painful to think about, but Ronald Reagan had the resilience of youth.

By 1935, broadcasting for WHO in Des Moines, Dutch Reagan was the head sportscaster and something of a local celebrity. Here he poses for an advertisement plugging pipe tobacco and cigarettes.

President Ronald Reagan, on a political tour, pays a nostalgic visit to WHO after fifty years, posing with an early microphone.

One evening he talked to his father about his frustrated radio ambitions. Jack loaned Dutch the old family heap, an Oldsmobile, and Ron took a swing around the Dixon area to nearby towns with stations to ask for work. First stop was WOC in Davenport, an hour's drive west, just over the Iowa state line.

Peter MacArthur, the station manager, an arthritic, crotchety Scotsman who walked with two canes, asked him caustically where he'd been? MacArthur had just hired a new announcer after advertising the job for a month.

Angry at his bad luck, Reagan burst out with a question: How the hell could a guy ever get to be a sports announcer if he couldn't get inside the station?

MacArthur told Ron to follow him down the hall to the studio. He sat the young man down in front of a microphone and told him to talk into it about football. MacArthur wanted to *see* the game as result of Ron's play descriptions.

The assignment was a snap for Ronald. For years at the frat house he'd entertained the guys by imitating a radio announcer, sometimes holding a broom upside down, pretending it was a mike on a stand, describing an imaginary football game play by play.

Love Is in the Air, Reagan's first film, started one week after he signed a movie contract on June 1, 1937. Most newly signed actors waited months before appearing in front of a camera. The girl in the movie is June Travis; Ronald's wise-cracking sidekick is Eddie Acuff.

As MacArthur listened, Ron dramatized an old Eureka game, made himself the hero, and built the story to a tense, last-second touchdown and victory.

MacArthur bought it. He offered Ronald five dollars and carfare to broadcast a University of Iowa game the following Saturday. If Dutch did well, he'd give him the next three home games at the same pay. At last Ronald Wilson Reagan of Dixon, Illinois, had his foot in the door.

That Saturday MacArthur listened closely to Ron's two-hour broadcast of the Iowa game, and he liked it. He immediately raised the novice announcer to ten dollars for the next three games. Then he sent Dutch home after the last game to wait his call for more work.

Two months went by; Christmas came and went. At last MacArthur called and hired Ronald as a permanent staff announcer at $100 a month! In 1933 this was a good salary, more than enough for Ron to live on his own in Davenport—enough to send money home to Jack and Nelle and to throw a spare ten once a month to Moon, who was still at Eureka.

Ronald Reagan in a 1938 publicity photo with Susan Hayward, with whom he was filming Girls on Probation. *Hayward was one of the few actresses (or actors) who didn't get along well with Ronald either on or off the sound stage.*

Now twenty-two, Ronald spent a year at WOC covering sports, doing interviews, reading commercials, and filling in as a disc jockey. One day WOC's sister station, WHO, a network affiliate in Des Moines, asked for Ronald. They heard a finished professional quality in his work and wanted him to cover track, football, and play-by-play re-creation of baseball games for a large Midwest audience.

At WHO he developed a superb talent for re-creating baseball games in the studio from raw data wired from the game by ticker tape. He dramatized the play-by-play events as if watching it all happen from the stadium press box. The engineer provided the roar-of-the-crowd sound effects.

By 1936 Ronald Reagan was making three times his starting salary: seventy-five dollars a week, twice the salary his father ever made. He was the Reagan family breadwinner. He regularly sent money home, increasing the sum after each raise. His parents needed Ron's help because Jack was in serious trouble. In his middle fifties, he'd suffered a series of near-fatal heart attacks, which made it impossible for him to ever work again.

From that time on, Ronald was the sole support of his parents. In later years he brought Nelle and Jack out to Los

Ronald had a lead role in Angels Wash Their Faces, *a sequel to* Angels with Dirty Faces, *a hit that starred James Cagney. The sequel was not a hit, but it was a romp for the Dead End Kids. The principal players are (from left to right)* Bonita Granville, Leo Gorcey, Gabe Dell, Reagan, Bobby Jordan, Huntz Hall, *and* Billy Halop. Seated is Henry O'Neill.

Angeles to live near him, and he gave them the deed to the first house they ever owned.

When Moon graduated, Dutch got him a job announcing at WOC.

After five years Ron was making ninety dollars a week. He was rich! He bought a new beige Nash convertible for cash and kept it for years, long after he could afford better as a contract actor in Hollywood.

He was happy doing sports on radio. But after five years, an old dream popped up every now and then—being an actor in the movies. He had an idea. In the spring of 1937 his WHO boss would be sending him again to Catalina Island, near Los Angeles, where he would cover the Chicago Cubs in spring training. Why not stop over in Hollywood on his way back to Des Moines? He could try calling one or two studios and see if he could get a break.

Two nights before he packed up to take the Los Angeles Limited, he and a secretary at WHO double-dated with another announcer and Joy Hodges, a Hollywood starlet and singer who had once worked at WHO. While they were dancing Ron told Joy about his movie ambitions. She told him to look her up when he got to Los Angeles. She would be glad to help.

It was the first week in April and Ronald had finished covering the Cubs in spring training on Catalina Island. Wearing his best blue suit, he went to the Biltmore Hotel in Los Angeles, where Joy Hodges was singing with Jimmy Grier's house band in the Biltmore Bowl. Joy waved to Ronald from the bandstand, pleased to see him again.

Sitting together during a break, he said he had come two thousand miles to take her up on her generous Des Moines offer. Would she still help him get into a studio?

"Sit tight," she said. She went out and called George Ward, her agent. "You have an appointment for tomorrow morning at the Bill Meiklejohn Agency," she said on returning. "Take off your glasses."

"I can't see," he protested as he removed them.

". . . and don't ever put them on again. You can't wear glasses in the movies."

Bill Meiklejohn liked Ron's earnest air and his innocence—but not the way he parted his hair in the middle. He called Max Arnow, Warner Brothers' chief casting director. Arnow could order a screen test for any new talent he liked.

"Max, I've got another Robert Taylor," Bill said.

"God only made one Robert Taylor," said Arnow, "but send him over."

Arnow saw the same appealing qualities Meiklejohn liked in Ron. He gave the young hopeful a scene from the Philip Barry play *Holiday* to memorize over the weekend. It was Friday; they would shoot the test on Monday. As Ron departed Arnow added, "We'll have to do something about your hair."

On Monday morning, having spent hours rehearsing with Joy on the weekend, he was sent first to studio makeup. The makeup specialists there parted his hair on the side, and it has remained that way ever since.

Today Ronald Reagan's estimation is that his screen test was a dog, but Arnow and Meiklejohn, watching him in the screening room, did not expect to see a finished actor. They found earnest, energetic, and wholesome qualities that showed up well on the screen. Ronald Reagan was the kind of attractive American archetype they could use. He looked like the young, clean-cut hero of a piece of fiction in the women's magazines.

"I'll show it to Jack Warner when he comes back from New York next week," said Arnow.

Ronald was in a bind. He couldn't wait that long. He had to go back to Des Moines to broadcast opening day of the baseball season. He left his Des Moines address with Bill Meiklejohn.

One week later a telegram from Meiklejohn asked Ron in Des Moines if he would accept a Warner's offer of two hundred a week and a seven-year contract. "Say yes," Ron wired back, "before they change their minds."

He quit his job, packed his bags, and bid Nelle, Jack, Moon, and all his friends farewell. He filled up his Nash convertible with nine-cents-a-gallon gasoline, and off he went on a three-day trip across the country to pursue his dream of becoming a movie star.

Ronald Reagan got off to a remarkably fast start in pictures. New players frequently languished for months before appearing in front of a camera. One week after Ron arrived, on June 1, 1937, he started at the very top of the low end of picture making. He played the lead in a B movie titled *Love Is in the Air*. It was a natural for Ronald, and the story explains why he was cast so quickly. He played a radio announcer who solves a murder by tricking racketeers into confessing their crime into an open microphone.

When the picture was ready for release, a meeting was held by the producer. What name should the studio give their new

An early publicity photograph of Reagan, taken between 1937 and 1939 by a studio photographer. At the studio's urgent request, he'd stopped parting his hair in the middle, as he had in his radio days.

performer? Ronald had introduced himself to everyone as Dutch Reagan. Brynie Foy, his producer, hated the name. They kicked around some first and last names. Suddenly Dutch Reagan realized he was about to lose his identity. He had a suggestion for them. How about Ronald Reagan? Yes, they said. It has a ring to it. Henceforth he would be known as Ronald Reagan.

He worked in eight B movies in a year. Three more times he was cast as an announcer, then as an attorney, a show business promoter, an insurance adjuster, a soldier, and a sports reporter. The forgettable gems include *Girls on Probation*, *Secret Service of the Air*, *Code of the Secret Service*, *Smashing the Money Ring*, and *Accidents Will Happen*.

Ronald Reagan's salary went up to five hundred a week.

Warner Brothers cast Ronald in a series of adventure movies starring him as a civilian pilot who joins the Secret Service. Here our hero battles one of the bad guys in the first of these films, Secret Service of the Air.

4
LIFE IN HOLLYWOOD
(1939–1940)

*D*espite the mediocrity of most of his pictures, Ronald Reagan's all-American guy quality was popular with audiences. The heavy fan mail and requests for his photo were a measure of audience approval that impressed the studio management.

Occasionally he was cast in a small part in an A movie—for example, *Dark Victory*, starring Bette Davis. But then he would find himself back in one of his B pictures. By 1940 he had moved up a couple of notches, appearing in small parts with Humphrey Bogart, Pat O'Brien, Edward G. Robinson, and James Cagney.

What impressed head producer Brynie Foy about Ronald Reagan were his dependability and steady work habits. In a tempestuous, emotionally chaotic business he showed up on time every day. He came in sober. Given his photographic memory, he always knew his lines perfectly. He had an easygoing disposition, took direction without tantrums, and was willing to accept small roles after playing better parts in A pictures. He did not demand to be made a top star. He did not complain about B pictures—steady money makers—being turned out as if on an assembly line with little attention to artistic merit. Studio publicity people always found him cooperative. He went, without complaint, on assigned dates with starlets to premieres, fancy restaurants, and nightclubs to promote his career or new film.

He never complained, because he saw himself as an apprentice working his way up to the top. He trusted that the studio would make him a star one day, so he resolved to take whatever came his way without objection.

His good-natured response came from his small-town view of life, and Warner's had a small-town atmosphere. He had lunch in the commissary with the Big Names every working day. He became friends with the top people he worked with, stars such as Dick Powell and Pat O'Brien, and he found nearly everybody as friendly as himself. He once called himself a sports announcer who came in awe to Hollywood. From childhood on he had been enveloped by the magic and illusion of the neighborhood theater. Even after he had built a career in the movies he never got over being awestruck at finding himself among those familiar film faces. They were the heroes he had looked up to in his youth.

Despite working in Hollywood, Ronald's private life was quiet, filled with small-town pursuits. He almost never went to nightclubs except for publicity purposes. He had a small apartment and he had his Nash to get around town. For a time, his parents and Neil, who had come to Los Angeles to work in radio, lived in an apartment around the corner, and they'd all go out to dinner together on weekends. He spent a lot of time riding horses as a member of the U.S. Cavalry Reserve. He swam in the ocean, took up golf, and spent time with a group of Des Moines bachelor friends who had come out to find a new life in California. Often he dated young starlets he met working in his pictures.

His strongest, most active interest was the Screen Actors Guild. He had joined the Guild, in part, to get acquainted with heroes from other studios. But he also liked meetings; he relished getting up in front of a crowd and speaking his mind. And he had an opinion on everything. He was on his feet two and three times a night.

He soon realized that he was working in a glorified factory, that the studios were not generous in their relations with the workers. What was needed was a strong actors' union to negotiate with management. Being compliant and submissive wasn't the way to get ahead. In terms of his own career, Ron was increasingly aware that the studio didn't seem to be interested in moving him up from B to A pictures—not without pressure.

He became skilled at negotiating with the studios on behalf of Guild members. He discovered that most negotiations did not go on during contract renewal time. Most involved enforcing contract terms on an everyday basis. The studios constantly tried to circumvent or ignore provisions they had agreed to. It was up to the Guild to keep them honest, and that meant daily battles.

Ronald actually enjoyed the rough and tumble of labor-management dealings. It was a little like football—there were offensive plays and defensive plays. There were end runs and plunges through the line, and the idea was still to win the game.

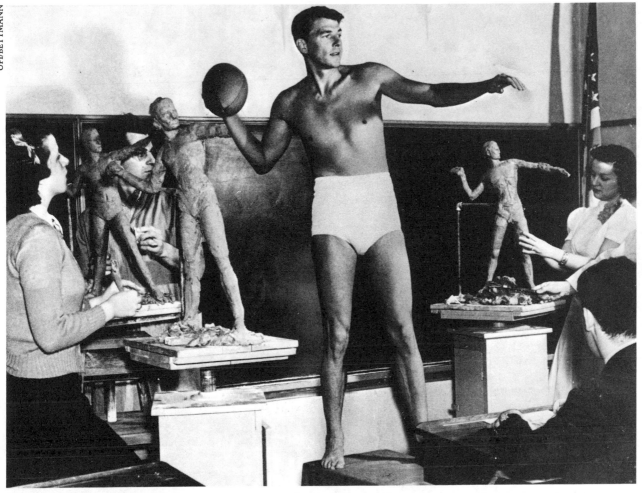

Ronald Reagan, early in his movie career, posing for a sculpting class at the University of Southern California. This was part of a Warner Brothers publicity scheme promoting Ronald as "Twentieth-Century Adonis with the most nearly perfect male figure in Hollywood."

If perhaps his movie career was pedestrian, Ronald Reagan's union career was vital and exciting. He was later elected president of the Screen Actors Guild six times. Hollywood may not have recognized him as an actor of first rank, but they did acknowledge him as a powerful Guild spokesman. He had rank, respect, and stature; he was a man to be reckoned with by the studios. He displayed character, determination, and grace under pressure; in his own quiet way he was beginning to reveal the qualities he sought in his own heroes.

The day he started on his ninth picture, *Brother Rat*, he met Jane Wyman. He had seen her around the studio before but had never spoken to her. A perky, pretty blonde who was bright and witty, she had been cast as his girl friend in the movie.

37

Reagan in the midst of a fake fight during a charity basketball game pitting actors against comedians. Here, Ronald, comedian Red Skelton, and actor Don McGuire battle for a loose ball.

Screen Actors Guild President Ronald Reagan as master of ceremonies at a benefit party for the poor of Los Angeles. Many stars performed, including Jimmy Cagney (in tuxedo), Charlie McCarthy as a Legionnaire, Edgar Bergen as a "swami."

Reagan, the star, besieged by fans at Grauman's Chinese Theater on Hollywood Boulevard during his second year in Movieland. His early movies were barely mediocre, but Ronald won a faithful following.

Ronald Reagan's first ranch, a modest eight acres near Van Nuys, was the setting for the young rancher shown here taking a hurdle on his favorite mount. This spread was the first of three Ronald has owned over the years.

39

For Reagan, ranching meant not only riding but hard, bracing work in the outdoors, a welcome change from the obligatory night-club hopping that every rising star was put through under the old-time studio system.

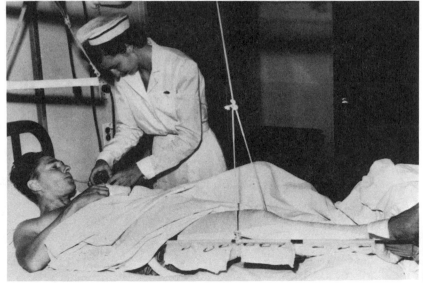

Ron Reagan spent six weeks in the hospital recovering from injuries sustained in a collision in a charity baseball game. He was laid up for months, and he came to his first date with actress Nancy Davis on crutches.

Reagan lunches at the studio commissary with actress Alexis Smith. They worked together in Ronald's first postwar movie, Stallion Road, in which Ronald, a veterinarian, becomes involved with Alexis, a rich lady who loves horses. Ron did his own riding and jumping in the film.

Ronald Reagan and actress Patricia Neal aboard the liner Queen Mary, on their way back to the States from England after working together on The Hasty Heart (1950).

With actress Ruth Roman, then an ingenue with Warner's, attending the American premiere of The Hasty Heart. *Attendance at the event was an exception for the twosome, who both preferred sporting events.*

Ronald and Jane Wyman visit the Brown Derby, famous watering place for Hollywood stars, tycoons and hangers-on, in 1939. This was a year after they first met on the set of Brother Rat, *and Jane was wearing Reagan's ring.*

The film was a comedy about a group of prankish, rowdy cadets in a military school, trying to graduate before they all got kicked out.

For Ronald Reagan, making the picture was great fun. It starred Eddie Albert, Priscilla Lane, Wayne Morris, and Ron and Jane. All young, up-and-coming actors destined for extended film careers, they carried on during the day on the set and at night after work.

Ronald found Jane, whom he decided he liked after one day of working together, a little standoffish. Married for a year to a dress manufacturer, she was going through a divorce.

Jane liked Ronald because he was sure of himself, extremely considerate, sentimental, and naïve. She, on the other hand, was distrustful and suspicious, hurt by a bad marriage.

Brother Rat was a hit. The studio decided to make a sequel with the same cast. Called *Brother Rat and a Baby*, the cast members all had another wild time making it. Unfortunately, the film failed to capture the verve and zaniness of the first picture, received poor reviews, and died a quiet death.

In late 1939 Jane and Ronald went on a nine-week publicity tour called *Stars of Tomorrow*, created by Louella Parsons. They had been going together for well over a year. When they reached Philadelphia they announced their engagement.

Ronald Reagan and Jane Wyman, the former Sarah Jane Faulks of St. Joseph, Missouri, were married on January 26, 1940. The ceremony was held at the Wee Kirk of the Heather Chapel at Forest Lawn in Glendale. A reception followed at Louella Parsons' home. She dubbed them a model Hollywood couple, and they tried to live up to the image.

5
STARRING
RONALD REAGAN:
A MOVIE ALBUM

Ronald Reagan's film career spanned twenty-six years (1938–1964), during which time he appeared in fifty-three movies. Most of his films were less than memorable, but Ronald was always a solid performer, with a certain charisma that made him an authentic movie star. His best work as a movie actor—and his best movies—came in the early forties, beginning with *Knute Rockne— All-American* (1940) and reaching its peak two years later with the release of *Kings Row*, which film historian Tony Thomas in his book, *Ronald Reagan: The Hollywood Years*, calls "the most distinguished film of Ronald Reagan's career and the one which drew him the most favorable response."

Presented here is a selective album of scenes from Reagan's most interesting and notable movies.

Reagan in a scene from Brother Rat, *his ninth picture and his best to date. It led to his meeting Jane Wyman, whom he subsequently married. Here, in the movie, Ronald discovers that Jane is beautiful when she takes off her glasses.*

Reagan's first important part in an A picture, although small, was in the famous Dark Victory, *made in 1939 and starring Bette Davis. In the movie, Ronald is a playboy and a drunk in love with Davis, who has no real interest in him. Reagan felt he didn't do his best work in the picture and believed he was poorly directed by the highly respected Edmund Goulding. Nonetheless, his appearance in* Dark Victory *propelled him toward stardom.*

Knute Rockne—All-American *was the making of Ronald Reagan as a movie star. He plays the part, comparatively small, of George Gipp, an outstanding collegiate football player from Notre Dame who dies tragically, murmuring to Coach Knute Rockne from his deathbed the immortal line: "Win one for the Gipper."*

Ronald Reagan, as George Gipp, getting the word from Coach Knute Rockne, played by Pat O'Brien. Years later, Pat O'Brien and Ronald Reagan received honorary degrees for their movie contribution to the glory of Notre Dame.

This is a scene from The Bad Man *(1941), in which Reagan starred with Wallace Beery, one of the great scene stealers in movie history. Reagan had been loaned out to MGM on the basis of good notices for his performance in* Knute Rockne—All-American. *The character played by Reagan is about to lose his ranch when Beery, playing a blustering border bandit whose life the Reagan character once saved, shows up to help him save the ranch.*

The film is Kings Row, *Ronald Reagan's favorite among all his films; Ann Sheridan and Reagan are shown in the key scene, where our hero discovers that his legs have been amputated by a sadistic doctor. He awakens from the operation and cries out, "Where's the rest of me?" The line was used as the title of his autobiography, published in 1965, shortly before he ran for governor of California.*

Juke Girl, *with Reagan and Ann Sheridan, shown here, was filmed in 1941, immediately after* Kings Row. *After their hard work in the previous film, the two stars didn't relish their roles in this earthy story of violence between struggling farmers and produce packers, set in Florida.*

The 1943 film version of This Is the Army, *based on a smash-hit Broadway production by Irving Berlin, was designed to raise money for war relief to benefit needy families of World War II servicemen. Ronald Reagan played the son of a World War I war hero (George Murphy). Everyone did this movie for love; Ronald made only his first lieutenant's wages of $250 per month. It was a welcome relief for Reagan, who, because of bad eyesight, was kept from active duty in the war and relegated to making training films on a studio lot.*

Ronald Reagan and Patricia Neal starred in John Loves Mary *(1949), a romantic farce about a returning World War II serviceman. John, played by Reagan, wins Mary but then loses her when he is obliged to marry a woman he doesn't love. He wins her back in the final reel.*

Shown again with Patricia Neal, this time in The Hasty Heart, *a 1950 movie set in a British military hospital in Burma, where Ronald plays the part of a recovering Yankee soldier and Patricia plays a nursing sister.*

The Hasty Heart, *one of Ronald's best pictures, also featured an outstanding performance by Richard Todd, a young British actor, as an embittered soldier who rejects the friendship of his fellow patients without realizing that he is terminally ill.*

54

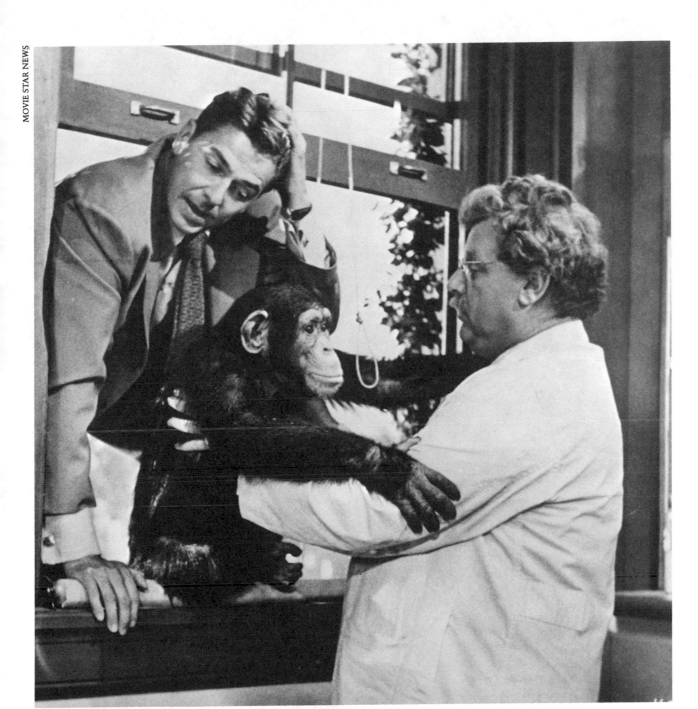

Bedtime for Bonzo *(1951), often ridiculed by Reagan's critics, is in actuality a charming comedy-romance about a college professor who takes over the rearing of an ape to prove an important point to his students. The stars were Reagan, Walter Slezak (pictured here with Bonzo), and Diana Lynn, but Ronald has admitted that the ape stole the picture.*

Cattle Queen of Montana *(1954) starred Ronald Reagan with Barbara Stanwyck in a fairly standard Western drama about an evil rancher manipulating the Blackfeet Indians to gain control of the herds owned by "the cattle queen," played by Stanwyck. Reagan, as an undercover army officer sent to investigate the Indian troubles, saves the day and wins the girl. Reagan enjoyed the chance to play opposite Barbara, known as a fine person to work with, and off the set, enjoyed riding in the beautiful country.*

Budding star Doris Day and Ronald Reagan played the leads in The Winning Team *(1952), the story of the legendary pitcher Grover Cleveland Alexander, who became a great baseball star, then hit bottom after a blow on the head brought on epilepsy and then alcoholism. Doris Day plays Alexander's loyal wife, who helped him in his spectacular comeback. Reagan has said that he regrets Warner Brothers' refusal to deal openly with the subject of epilepsy in the film.*

Reagan plays a quick-drawing cowhand in Tennessee's Partner, *set in a rough-and-ready mining town. The film, released in 1955, also starred John Payne, Rhonda Fleming, and Coleen Gray. It may have been the most effective Western Ronald Reagan ever made.*

Hellcats of the Navy *(1957), a dramatization of a real-life naval operation in the Pacific against the Japanese, was neither a box-office nor an artistic success and may have led to Ronald Reagan's departure from the film business. There was one positive result: It let Ronald work with Mrs. Reagan. The two are shown here with costar Arthur Franz.*

6

THE MIDDLE YEARS: MARRIAGE, WAR, DIVORCE, SCREEN ACTORS GUILD (1940–1948)

For Jane Wyman and Ronald Reagan, living in a house in West Hollywood meant being constantly in the public eye.

Like most newly married couples in the 1940s, they wanted to have children as soon as possible. "Hollywood's happiest couple," as they were dubbed by the press, got their wish a year after they were wed: a daughter, Maureen Elizabeth, born on January 4, 1941. Ronald hoped to add a son, but Jane's evolving career made having another child impractical. Finally, in March of 1945, the couple brought home a four-day-old adopted infant boy, Michael Edward Reagan.

In April of 1942, five months after Pearl Harbor, Ronald was called into the army. He was a reserve officer in the cavalry, having joined back in the days when he was a broadcaster in Des Moines so he could learn to ride a horse, and the call was expected.

Ronald had made twenty-eight movies by the time he went into the army. Two, *Knute Rockne—All American* and *Kings Row*, both A pictures, had given him important acting credits and brought him a substantial raise. His performance in *Kings Row* enabled his agent, Lew Wasserman, to renegotiate a contract at $3500 a week, three times his old salary, before the picture was even in release. Ronald gave a first-rate performance as a young playboy who loses his money, goes to work in a railroad yard, has an accident, and is treated by a sadistic doctor who amputates both of his legs. The line the young man cries out in shock and despair when he discovers he is an amputee, "Where's the rest of me?", is famous today, and the scene itself is unforgettable. The line is also the title of Ronald Reagan's autobiography, written twenty-three years after the release of *Kings Row* in 1942. Ronald believed the fine reviews and the success of *Kings Row* would assure him first-rank stardom when he returned from the service.

Because of his poor eyesight, he was put on limited stateside service all through the war. An army doctor, testing his vision upon arrival at Fort Mason near San Francisco, the actor's first military assignment, remarked that if they sent him overseas with a gun he'd probably shoot a general—"ours." "And he'd probably miss him," added another doctor.

The Army Air Corps, needing experienced film specialists, shipped Ronald back to Los Angeles after he had spent several months at Fort Mason overseeing supplies being loaded onto transports for the Pacific and helping arrange entertainment on the base. He was assigned to the First Air Force Motion Picture Unit at the Hal Roach studios in Culver City. Most of his work was narrating training films, documentaries, and newsreels, but he was also released for several weeks to return to his old studio, Warner Brothers, to make Irving Berlin's *This Is the Army*, whose proceeds went to army relief work.

Fort Wacky, as the Roach studio was called, wasn't the army we all know. The Hollywood-bred GI's in their olive drab uniforms and two-tone shoes went home every weekend after work, and their antics were right out of a Hollywood screwball comedy.

One day soon after he arrived, Lieutenant Reagan, in a military mood, decided to shape up his ragged unit to look like something the United States army could be proud of. He took the lackadaisical outfit out to the field and put them through close-order drill. After he had finished marching their legs off, three lowly privates came over to their commander and told him in blunt army language never to do that again. They reminded Ronald that although he was an officer, he was also an actor, and while they were lowly privates, they were also producers and directors. After the war they were going to be producers and directors again, and he hoped to be an actor again. Right? That was the end of close-order drill at Fort Wacky.

Ronald was discharged with the rank of captain in late 1945 when the war ended. He immediately returned to Warner Brothers for a visit, expecting things to be as he had left them, only to discover that some critical changes had occurred. The tragic experiences of war had created a more sophisticated audience. New young stars had become the public's favorites, and the new and younger audiences had never heard of Ronald Reagan. He

Jane Wyman and Ronald Reagan at their wedding reception after the January 26, 1940, ceremony at the Wee Kirk o'the Heather, a Hollywood institution. Louella Parsons, one of the most powerful figures in Movieland at the time, was the hostess of the reception, dubbing the newlyweds "a model couple," a role they did their best to live up to.

The young Reagans in the kitchen of their Sunset Plaza apartment above the famous Sunset Strip, having a late-night snack shortly after their marriage.

Jane Reagan salutes the newly commissioned Lieutenant Reagan, who, because of his nearsightedness, was soon to find himself back on a studio lot christened Fort Wacky by the actors, directors, and technicians who worked there for the war effort.

was going to have to establish himself all over again with movie audiences.

Convincing the studio that he needed a vehicle to make his comeback, Ronald was cast in *Stallion Road*, a mediocre Warner Brothers production with Alexis Smith and Zachary Scott. His second film, *That Hagen Girl*, a love story in which he costarred with Shirley Temple, he did as a favor to the studio, although he knew the script was weak. Using Ronald, who was twenty years older than his costar, as Shirley Temple's lover was poor casting. It was becoming clear to him that Warner's was using him poorly, and he found himself in a constant battle with the studio. The small-town community feeling that he had loved as an up-and-coming actor was gone forever.

Nineteen forty-seven was a troubled year for the Reagan family. In June Jane lost an infant girl, born four months prematurely. While Jane was recovering, Ronald went into the hospital for a severe bout of viral pneumonia. For a time his doctor wasn't certain he'd survive, but a determined nurse stayed by his bedside, coaxing him to take breath after breath until the crisis

Ronald, the proud father, with baby Maureen, one year old (born January 4, 1941), and wife, Jane. He was about to leave for active duty.

was past. To this day Ronald Reagan gives her the credit for inspiring him with the will to live.

In 1947 Ronald was elected president of the Screen Actors Guild for the first time. His Guild work began to fill all his available time when he wasn't acting at the studio. When the Guild became embroiled in a tough jurisdictional strike between two studio craft unions, he was drawn in even deeper. At one point he was warned that if he made a certain investigative report public, someone would fix his face so he would never work in pictures again. The threat, he wrote in his autobiography, seemed genuine, and he both carried a gun for a time and received police protection for himself and his family.

The battle between left- and right-wing factions over union control aroused the attention of the House Un-American Activities Committee, which came to Hollywood looking for Communists, armed with a blacklist that split the movie community into hostile camps.

A postwar Reagan family photo, showing Ronald, Maureen, young Michael (adopted in March 1945), and Jane. The intense publicity focused on them in this period may well have helped create the strains that threatened the marriage.

With (from left to right) screen stars Robert Montgomery and George Murphy, leaving the Capitol in Washington, D.C., on October 23, 1947, following testimony before the House Un-American Activities Committee. Ronald Reagan, as a result of experiences with Communist sympathizers in the Screen Actors Guild, had become increasingly conservative in his political views.

Testifying before the House Committee, Ronald Reagan, attacked the pro-Communist element in Hollywood but told the committee he would hesitate to outlaw any political party because of its views, a libertarian position that jolted some committee members.

Ronald was called before the committee in Washington to testify about Communists in the movie industry. By now the liberalism he had learned from his father had been tempered by postwar experiences with Hollywood radicals willing to accommodate avowed or covert Communists inside the movie industry. He had quit two new postwar liberal organizations, the American Veterans Committee and the Independent Committee for the Arts, Sciences and Professions, declaring them Communist fronts. In Washington he testified to his abhorrence of their political tactics.

While Ronald deeply involved himself in Guild work, Jane's career was on the rise in a spectacular way. Once known for her light comedy roles, she was now succeeding in serious dramatic roles in such major films as *Lost Weekend* and *The Yearling*. She was nominated for an Academy Award for the latter, and the following year she won the Academy Award for her brilliant portrayal of a deaf-mute in *Johnny Belinda*. Her once casual attitude toward acting had turned serious.

After seven years, Jane and Ronald's marriage began to come apart, partly because of strains caused by her career being on the rise while his was going nowhere and partly because of his increasing involvement in union work. Jane, struggling with the tensions of her work, displayed little interest in Ronald's intense preoccupation with Guild politics. He, on the other hand, thought her acting and studio problems were not serious, could easily be solved by compromise, and were simply not worth worrying about.

There had been no real communication between the two for a long time. They disagreed on discipline of the children—she

Actors George Murphy, Robert Montgomery, chief committee counsel Robert Stripling, and Ronald Reagan confer over their upcoming appearance before a session of the House of Representatives un-American Activities Committee investigating alleged Communist influence in the movie industry.

In early October of 1947, a large group of screen stars, members of the Screen Actors Guild, attended an emergency meeting to discuss a strike against the film studios. Shown here (from left to right) are Jane Wyman, Henry Fonda, Boris Karloff, and Gene Kelly. Ronald Reagan, standing, was a major force in the ultimate decision.

favored firmness; he was more casual—which led to additional conflict.

Jane asked for a divorce, and they separated in December of 1947. There was a week's try at reconciliation before the actual divorce on June 28, 1948, but that failed. Jane received custody of Maureen, age seven, and Michael, age three, plus child support and half the community property, worth $75,000. Ronald did not contest the divorce, although he never truly wanted it.

7
NANCY
(1949)

One fall day in 1949 Ronald Reagan received a call at home from Mervyn LeRoy, a top MGM director. He hoped Mervyn was calling to offer him a part, but this was Guild business. Nancy Davis, a starlet working in LeRoy's *East Side, West Side*, had found her name on lists of accused Communist-front organizations and on left-wing petitions. Fearing she was going to end up on a Hollywood blacklist, she had asked if LeRoy would call the Screen Actors Guild president for his help. Ronald, as a favor to the director, agreed to look into the problem personally.

Nancy Davis, a twenty-eight-year-old former Broadway actress, had come to Hollywood in 1947 and signed a seven-year MGM contract. She was born Anne Francis Robbins in Manhattan in 1921. Her father and mother were not getting along, and not long after Anne's birth Ken Robbins left the marriage permanently.

Anne Francis' mother had acted on Broadway, performing under her maiden name, Edith Luckett, and returned to her career after Ken Robbins left her. At first Edith took baby Anne on tour with her, but she found she couldn't simultaneously manage a hectic life on the road and raise a growing child. When Anne Francis was two, Edith asked her oldest sister, Virginia, and Virginia's husband, Audley Galbraith, to raise the girl in Bethesda, Maryland, while Edith pursued her career.

Anne Francis' surrogate parents were as warm and giving to her as they were to their own daughter, Charlotte, who was Nancy's age. The family was well-to-do, so Anne Francis had all she ever needed in life, although she was frequently lonely for her real mother and father.

Edith Luckett often visited her daughter in Bethesda, bringing presents for Anne Francis and Charlotte. A flamboyant, slightly outrageous woman, Edith dressed in elegant clothes and told wonderful stories about her stage friends, among whom she numbered Walter Huston, Zasu Pitts, and Colleen Moore.

Finally tiring of the stage six years after she had left Anne Francis with her sister, Edith gave up acting to marry Dr. Loyal Davis, a distinguished and wealthy neurosurgeon. Eight-year-old Anne Francis was the flower girl at her mother's wedding, held in May of 1929, and joyfully went to live with her mother and stepfather in Chicago. Dr. Davis was a man of great charm—a gentle father but also a strict disciplinarian who insisted Anne Francis learn proper manners. Anne Francis grew up to be much more like her new, reserved "father" than her mother. When she was fourteen, Davis asked Anne Francis if she wanted to be adopted by him. Yes, she said, but she had to get her natural father's permission. She went to get Ken Robbins' consent for her adoption by Dr. Davis and the change of her name legally to Nancy Davis. He did not show it, but Ken Robbins took Nancy's rejection of him very hard. It was the last time she saw her natural father.

The Davis family lived in luxury on Chicago's exclusive Shore Drive. Nancy was enrolled in the fashionable Girls' Latin School, made her debut, and went to Smith College, where she majored in dramatics. Upon graduation she went to New York to make her fortune in the Broadway theater. She worked in several plays, including *Lute Song* with Mary Martin, and toured in *The Late Christopher Bean* with her mother's old friend, Zasu Pitts.

Supported in part by her parents, she did not have to scramble to pay the rent, unlike most young actresses in New York making their way in the theater in the 1940s. But like most neophyte actresses she did find it difficult getting work in the theater and had to turn to part-time modeling of hats as a Conover model. A blind date with Benny Thau, a vice-president of MGM who had seen her in a small television part, brought an invitation to come out to Hollywood to take a screen test for MGM. When the blacklist problem came up, she had made two B pictures, *Shadow on the Wall* and *The Doctor and the Girl*.

Ronald called Mervyn LeRoy back with news that Nancy Davis was being confused with another actress of the same name. She need not worry. If trouble came, the Guild would be at her side.

Anne Francis Robbins, about age two, in an undated photograph from the White House archives. It was at about this time that her mother, Edith, was forced by circumstances to leave Nancy in the care of Edith's older sister in Bethesda, Maryland.

Edith Luckett, Nancy's mother, in her younger days as an actress on Broadway and in summer stock. One can see the resemblance between mother and daughter around the eyes and mouth.

Dr. Loyal Davis, a prominent Chicago neurosurgeon, married Nancy's mother in 1929; Nancy was a flower girl at the wedding. Dr. Davis was probably the most important influence in Nancy's early life, and when she was fourteen he legally adopted her.

But, Nancy protested to LeRoy, shouldn't she hear it from the SAG president personally? Couldn't they discuss it over dinner? The truth was, Nancy Davis had fallen for the handsome actor on the screen and was attracted by all she'd read about his leadership qualities as head of the Guild.

Ron understood the subliminal message delivered by LeRoy. He agreed to call Nancy. She at least had to be pretty if she was a starlet under contract to MGM.

They talked cautiously on the phone about dinner, keeping up the facade about the blacklist, agreeing they would make their meeting brief because they both had an early call at the studio the next day—not true in either case.

Ronald, injured a short time before in a charity baseball game, made his way up the stairs to Nancy's second floor apartment with the aid of two canes. What he saw when the apartment door opened were the largest, softest, and most gentle eyes he had ever seen.

The "short dinner" at LaRue's lasted two hours, with Ronald keeping up a steady stream of conversation about politics, sports, Hollywood gossip, and Guild matters. Nancy sat in rapt attention. Dinner was followed by a trip to see Sophie Tucker at Ciro's; they sat through two shows, and ended up on the lady's doorstep at 3:00 A.M. If a columnist had been around that night, the story would have been short and simple: These two were genuinely taken with each other.

Nancy Davis, nearly thirty, was ready to marry and raise a family. She had no illusions about becoming a star—"I was never a career woman," she admitted in later years—hoping instead for a successful and happy marriage. When she married Ronald Reagan, her true career began.

But a newly divorced Ronald Reagan hadn't the slightest interest in another permanent alliance with any woman. That didn't mean they couldn't carry on a leisurely courtship. In fact, that went on for two years, with both Ronald and Nancy dating other people during that time.

When Reagan brought Nancy to visit the new 350-acre ranch at Malibu Lake that he had purchased in the summer of 1951, he found that her company deeply enhanced his enjoyment of ranch life. It pleased him that she got on well with his children, Maureen and Michael, when they came up on weekend visits to the ranch. Being with Nancy and his kids evoked warm feelings and the contentment of family life that he had sorely missed.

Sitting beside his friend Bill Holden at a meeting one day, Ronald wrote a note and handed it to Bill. "To hell with this,"

At Smith College, Nancy Davis puts up a poster for a 1943 theatrical production in Northampton, Massachusetts. She is remembered by a classmate as being "a big movie fan and devoted to acting."

The twenty-eight-year-old Nancy Davis in a studio publicity photograph made two years after she was signed to a movie contract by MGM. She'd had parts in two movies when she met handsome actor Ronald Reagan.

Nancy Davis in The Glamor Girl, *another 1943 Smith College production. She is in the center "getting a kick" out of a pair of her classmates. A college friend "wasn't at all surprised to see her in Hollywood."*

Screen star William Holden (extreme right) was best man at Ronald Reagan's wedding to Nancy Davis on March 4, 1952. Brenda Marshall (Mrs. Holden) was the matron of honor. Holden, a great admirer of Nancy, had told his good friend Ronald, "It's about time!"

The happy duo make the first cut together into the three-tiered wedding cake.

Jack Benny, George Burns, Frank Sinatra, and the Reagans meet at a Hollywood soirée. The photo is undated, but the year was probably 1953.

The happily married Reagans at their ranch. Nancy has since joked,
"He married me to get the fences painted."

The First Lady arrives in her "second hand clothes" to perform at Washington's Gridiron Club. Welcoming her to the event is club vice-president Charles McDowell.

Nancy Reagan clowns with television's Mr. T. at a White House Christmas ceremony, to which the star of "The A Team" came dressed as Santa Claus.

Nancy with son, Ron, riding around the White House grounds on a bicycle built for two, with Ron doing the clowning and Nancy doing all the work.

The First Lady with her mother, Edith Luckett Davis. The occasion was the awarding of the Arizona Lifetime Achievement Award for Mrs. Davis's work with the retarded.

First ladies, past and present, attend 1982 funeral services for Bess Truman, widow of former President Harry S. Truman. From left are: Nancy Reagan, Betty Ford, and Rosalynn Carter.

The president and Nancy Reagan supping informally in the study of the family quarters of the White House.

WHITE HOUSE

it read. "How would you like to be best man when I marry Nancy?"

"It's about time!" Holden exclaimed, and the two men got up and walked out.

On March 4, 1952, Nancy Davis and Ronald Reagan were married at the Little Brown Church in the Valley, with Bill Holden as best man and his wife, Brenda Marshall, as matron of honor.

After the wedding, the couple moved into Nancy's apartment in Westwood. They lived there until they found a $24,000 four-bedroom ranch-style house in Pacific Palisades. Today Pacific Palisades is an exclusive and wealthy area, but at that time it was sparsely populated and rather far from Hollywood for an actor. But it had the small-town atmosphere Ronald wanted and a stunning view of the Pacific. Besides that, it was less than an hour's drive to his ranch near Lake Malibu.

It wasn't long before the couple had started their own family. Patricia Ann Reagan was born by caesarean section on October 22, 1952. They also wanted a boy, but Nancy subsequently suffered several miscarriages. On her doctor's advice, she spent the last three months of a later pregnancy in bed and on May 20, 1958, gave birth by caesarean section to Ronald Prescott Reagan, Jr.

In 1956 things were going well for the Reagans. Ronald was earning $150,000 a year as host of "GE Theatre," and he built a new home on a high bluff in Pacific Palisades. They lived there for twenty-four years, selling the house only when they moved into the White House in 1981.

Through the best and worst of times, after thirty-five years of marriage, Ronald and Nancy are now as much in love as they were the day they married. The proof is there for every American to see in the adoring glances they give to each other so often, as recorded in our newspapers, magazines, and on television.

8

FROM "GE THEATRE" HOST TO GOVERNOR (1950–1966)

There was trouble in Hollywood. Box office receipts at movie theaters began to drop off. Between 1947 and 1951, profits at Warner Brothers, Ronald Reagan's studio, dropped from $22 million to $9 million. The sale of television sets in America almost doubled annually, and the old film-going public began skipping the traditional Sunday night at the movies, staying home instead.

Movie actor Ronald Reagan and his fellow Guild members had to face being out of work as motion picture production was cut back severely.

Ronald Reagan's movie days were on the wane, although he did make fifty-two pictures in a twenty-year career that lasted from 1937 to 1957. His final picture, *Hellcats of the Navy*, starred Ron as a naval commander and Nancy as nurse and leading lady. It was the only movie they made together. "I must say the love scenes were the easiest I ever had to do," she commented years later.

But the last years as a film star were difficult. By 1954 Ronald was in financial straits, trying to keep up the home in Pacific Palisades and his ranch at Lake Malibu. He had made just one picture a year from 1951 to 1954, including the now notorious *Bedtime for Bonzo* (1951).

Hoping to find some way his client could earn money, Ronald's agent, Lew Wasserman of MCA, suggested Las Vegas.

MCA worked out an offer with the Last Frontier. For two weeks' work Ronald would receive as much money as he made for an entire movie. The show, comedy with singing and dancing, was a success and brought impressive offers to appear at the Waldorf in New York, nightclubs in Miami and Chicago, and the London Palladium. Ronald turned them down because he and Nancy didn't like the boredom, the wasted hours spent in hotel rooms waiting for the nightly performance. Besides that, they missed the children, home, and friends.

One day Taft Shrieber, head of MCA's Revue Productions, asked Ron if he'd like to host television's "General Electric Theatre," a very successful Sunday night half-hour dramatic anthology, at a salary of $150,000 a year. The one embellishment on the usual contract offer was a proviso that Ronald Reagan would also tour the country for ten weeks promoting GE products, visiting GE plants, and meeting managers and workers.

The day he took the camera test for the job as host for "General Electric Theatre" he gave it his very best. A perfect fit as host—smooth, attractive, and convincing—Ronald also proved a superb product salesman for GE.

For ten weeks a year, Ronald toured GE plants across the country, meeting executives at lunch, shaking hands, and visiting with the employees. He suggested making a brief speech before the groups and developed a basic short talk that included Hollywood stories and one-line jokes.

He gradually expanded his talk in a way that would have a remarkable effect on his later life. He began tailoring his remarks to reflect the GE executives' attitudes, watching their responses and refining his presentation accordingly. Picking up on their social and political concerns, he began to discuss wasteful spending, federal regulations, taxes, and bureaucracy, meanwhile praising personal initiative as the American way. His basic GE speech, as it became known over the years, turned into a small masterpiece, combining conservative politics and the American frontier spirit. This impressed the executives at the 135 GE plants across the country. Reagan won their respect. In turn, their acceptance of him solidified the political views he espoused, which grew more firmly conservative the longer he remained on the GE program.

All went well during the term of President Eisenhower, a Republican, but when John F. Kennedy was elected in 1960, Ronald Reagan's conservative views became a problem for GE. Ronald modified his company speech, but his outspoken conservatism, espoused before conservative groups on the banquet circuit, became an increasingly sticky matter for the company. One day a GE executive called him at home with an order

In 1954, when things were bad in Hollywood, Ronald Reagan, in order to pay his bills, took a job as host on the popular TV show "General Electric Theatre," also signing on as goodwill ambassador for GE products. The speeches he made around the country led him very soon from show business to politics.

In February 1954, seeking to reinvigorate his career, Ronald Reagan did a two-week stint in Las Vegas, playing with the Continentals, a slapstick team of singers and dancers, at the Ramona Room of the Last Frontier Hotel. His fellow performers praised Ronald as a quick learner and nimble dancer. Nancy, who sat for hours through rehearsals and performances, was acclaimed a great trouper.

After his conservative viewpoint forced him to leave GE, Reagan worked as host and sometimes a performer (see above) in "Death Valley Days," but he found the work unsatisfying.

Ronald Reagan's television speech in the final days of the losing Goldwater presidential campaign in 1964 was a smash hit, and Senator
Goldwater (left) yielded the mantle of leading Republican conservative
to the former actor from California.

Urged on by two wealthy businessmen, Ronald Reagan at fifty-
four launched himself on the
campaign trail in 1966, running
against the incumbent, Pat
Brown, for the governorship of
California.

In San Diego, at a rally of "Mexican-Americans for Reagan," the fledg-
ling politician wins voters while trying on a sombrero.

In San Jose, at a Mexican Independence Day parade, candidate Reagan good-naturedly survived booing from the crowd along the way.

henceforth to stick strictly to selling GE products. Irked, Reagan refused. Two weeks later GE accepted his resignation, and "GE Theatre," whose Sunday ratings had fallen behind its competition, "Bonanza," was cancelled. Back in television the next season as the apolitical host of "Death Valley Days," Ronald found it dull stuff after GE.

Meanwhile, after losing the presidency to John F. Kennedy in 1960, Richard M. Nixon decided to run for governor of California against Pat Brown. Ronald, a registered Democrat whose conservative views were by now well known, agreed to campaign for Nixon. He also decided it was time to reregister as a Republican.

He was finished as leading man on the big screen. At fifty-three, his future on the small screen was also questionable, and it wasn't in him to become an aging character actor.

Ron and Nancy both agreed his future lay in politics. Through his brother, Moon Reagan, who was involved in the Goldwater campaign for president against Lyndon Johnson in 1964, Ronald was made cochairman of the Citizens for Goldwater-Miller Committee. Goldwater was to lose by a landslide, but what followed for Ronald Reagan was another story.

Goldwater's national campaign team decided to let Reagan make a last-ditch speech on national television, the actor's first, urging people to vote for Goldwater. Entitled "A Time for Choosing," the address was a polished reworking of Reagan's famous GE speech, essentially antigovernment, denouncing communism and celebrating individual freedom. He spoke of the great

At a first encounter with Governor Pat Brown on NBC-TV's "Meet the Press," Ronald lambasted leftist Democratic policies, while Brown claimed Reagan's policies would harm the man in the street.

Ronald and Nancy Reagan emerge from the voting booth after casting ballots in the Republican primary. Reagan handily defeated former San Francisco Mayor George Christopher, damaged by a political maneuver by Governor Brown, who preferred to run against an ex-actor than against a seasoned politico.

future of America. He attacked the growth of "big government" and asserted a need to give initiative back to the American people. He offered straightforward solutions to what seemed to be overwhelming problems.

Encouraging his audience to look to the future of America with faith and optimism, Reagan quoted his erstwhile hero, Franklin Roosevelt: "You and I have a rendezvous with destiny. We will preserve for our children this, the last best hope for man on earth, or we will sentence them to take the last step into a thousand years of darkness."

Reagan's attractive qualities of honesty and earnestness shone through. "The one bright spot in a dismal campaign," said *Time.* In just one night, the movie actor and political neophyte succeeded Goldwater as standard-bearer for the nation's conservative voters.

Ronald Reagan had transformed himself from a celebrity at the end of his acting career into the nation's most important conservative politician. He brought in $1 million in contributions to the party, more money than had ever been raised by a political speech up to that time.

The immediate outcome was a visit to Reagan's home in Pacific Palisades by two wealthy southern California businessmen and political king-makers. Holmes Tuttle, an auto dealer, and Henry Salvatori, an oil man, asked him to run for governor on the Republican ticket in 1966 against the Democratic incumbent, Pat Brown.

Reagan agreed to become the candidate if the two men could show both that they had the money and that he had the support

On a visit to former President Eisenhower in Gettysburg, gubernatorial candidate Reagan got sage advice from Ike and much attention from newsmen.

Governor-elect Ronald Reagan receiving congratulations over the phone.

Nancy Reagan watches Ronald take the oath of office as thirty-third governor of California. His early days in his first elective office were somewhat rocky, but Reagan, as usual, proved to be a fast learner.

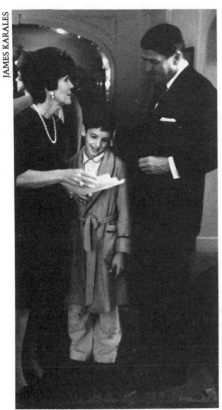

Governor Reagan's residence in Sacramento. The Reagans moved here after the governor's mansion, a Victorian relic, proved rundown and unsafe.

At a gubernatorial reception, young Ron, Jr., in bedclothes, crashes the party and receives loving attention from Nancy and Ronald Reagan.

Then a New York senator, the late Robert F. Kennedy debated long-distance with Governor Ronald Reagan on a CBS-TV news program aired May 15, 1967.

Governor Reagan escorts President-elect Richard Nixon across the field at half-time at the 1969 Rose Bowl game between the University of Southern California and Ohio State.

of key political leaders in the state. Thus encouraged, the two men organized a "Friends of Ronald Reagan" fund and hired the best political public relations firm in California, Spencer and Roberts. The campaign was on!

In January of 1966, following a four-month speechmaking tour around the state, Ronald Reagan announced his candidacy for governor of California. His first objective was to defeat George Christopher, the former mayor of San Francisco, in the Republican primaries. After that he would take on Democrat Pat Brown, who was running for a third term.

Ronald beat Christopher in June of 1966 by a whopping 64 percent of the vote. It was to be a Reagan versus Brown contest in September.

Pat Brown underestimated Ronald Reagan. (Throughout his political career, Reagan's opponents have erred in seeing him as an easy mark.) Brown fully expected the novice candidate to make a critical mistake under the pressure of questioning by reporters, but such a goof never happened. In fact, Reagan became friendly with the press, and that worked to his advantage.

Brown also overestimated his own popularity. He kept emphasizing past accomplishments, which the voters weren't interested in hearing about. They were worried about taxes and rising inflation.

Faltering at the start, Reagan recovered and, drawing on his eight-year GE background, deftly handled questions from newsmen and the public. He was pleasant and highly articulate. Even reporters who disliked his politics liked the man himself.

Reagan came up with some strong positions: People were too dependent on the government, which controlled the people instead of the people controlling the government; government was too bureaucratic and too expensive; taxes had to come down; government regulations had a choke hold on American business.

Brown, it turned out, was a tired man after eight years in office. There was no fire in his campaign. Moreover, he made a serious mistake, demeaning Ronald Reagan as "an actor." It never occurred to Brown's people that California was a state in which people thought more highly of actors than of politicians! By August, a month before the election, "the actor" was leading in the Gallup polls by 11 percent, and on election day Reagan beat Brown by a million votes. Ronald Wilson Reagan, an ex-actor who had never won an election or held political office in his life, was governor of the great state of California.

9

GOVERNOR OF CALIFORNIA AND CANDIDATE FOR THE PRESIDENCY (1968–1978)

Ronald Reagan was sworn in as California's thirty-third governor at one minute after midnight on January 2, 1967, in the state capital of Sacramento.

"Well, Murphy," he said to Senator George Murphy, his old pal from movie days, "here we are on 'The Late Late Show' again."

Ronald and Nancy had to give up their privacy in a way they hadn't experienced as actors. Reagan took it in stride, but it was difficult for Nancy, who was essentially a private person.

Trained from childhood by Dr. Loyal Davis to prize good manners, Nancy inherently disliked the rough-and-tumble world of politics. Wanting to help Ron in his career, she made public speeches but found doing so painful and a strain on her nerves.

Their refuge from the world had been the ranch, where life's problems disappeared after a day in the hills and woods, riding the trails and working around the house. But then that, too, came to an end.

"It's a family joke that Ronnie married me just to get someone to paint the fences. We put a lot of ourselves into the place.

But as governor he had to take a large cut in income. We simply could not afford the luxury of a ranch." On the other hand, since the Reagans sold the ranch for $2 million, they were now financially secure as they had never been before.

The governor's mansion in Sacramento overlooked a filling station, an all-night cocktail lounge, and a very active American Legion hall. Built in 1879, fifty years of California governors had lived in the four-story Victorian house, which resembled a set for a Gothic murder mystery. The place was filled with dry rot and had been condemned as a fire hazard years earlier, with the use of all seven attractive fireplaces ruled out.

Nancy moved into the mansion reluctantly. The Reagans knew they couldn't move without causing a political furor, but then came the day Nancy Reagan said, politics or no politics, they were getting out. She had tried to show Ron Jr. how to escape from his second floor bedroom in the event a fire started, but neither the screen nor the window would open. When she asked the fire marshall for his advice, he said, "Tell your son to pull out one of the dresser drawers. Have him hold it out in front of him, run toward the window, break the glass, and climb out. He'll be safe on the roof." That did it for the governor's lady.

The Reagans rented a large, beautiful two-story Tudor house on the outskirts of town, with a fireplace that worked and a huge backyard with trees and a swimming pool, where they could hold outdoor parties. Even though they paid the rent on the new house out of their own pocket, moving caused a political furor in the legislature, as they'd expected. But it also served a purpose, prompting the state finally to build a new governor's mansion, which the Reagans never occupied.

Two years later, on a hunt around the Santa Ynez Mountains near Santa Barbara, the Reagans found a large, deserted ranch. Once more, Ronald began working with his own hands at turning a piece of country land into a ranch and retreat. A dozen years later Rancho del Cielo would become famous as the president's refuge from White House cares.

The open secret about Ronald Reagan was that Nancy was his source of support and inspiration. He would never have become governor without her—nor president. She made home serene, the way he liked it, kept intruders at arm's length, made sure he got his rest, fixed the food he liked to eat, and arranged his appointments so he had time to watch his favorite television shows. She was indispensable to his well-being and health and shared his daily problems as confidante.

"My life fell into place when I married him. He gave me security and peace of mind and love. I wasn't looking for any more. I had it."

Gubernatorial fan mail amounted to about 100,000 letters in just two months after Ronald Reagan took office in January 1967.

Nancy Reagan took charge of redecorating the new California governor's offices in Sacramento, introducing an "Old California" theme.

UPI/BETTMANN

At the Republican National Convention in Miami in August 1968, Ronald Reagan was warmly welcomed by delegates, but he and Nelson Rockfeller lost the nomination to Richard Nixon on the first ballot.

UPI/BETTMANN

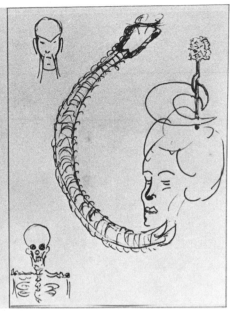

Armchair psychologists could have a field day with this Ronald Reagan doodle, done while attending a Western Governors' Conference in Honolulu, Hawaii, in May 1968.

Ronald Reagan, with Nancy in the foreground, receives "favorite son" support in Anaheim, California, though to no avail.

Governor Ronald Reagan fires a perfect spiral to Speedy Duncan (far right) of the San Diego Chargers as players from the San Francisco 49ers and the Los Angeles Rams watch in admiration. The occasion was to honor them for their work in the summer-jobs-for-youth program.

Christmas 1969 with the Reagans at their Pacific Palisades home. Patti, Ronald, Ron, Jr., and Nancy gather in front of a festive tree. Governor Reagan, in a message to Californians, asked them to join in praying for "the miracle that lies within the meaning of Christmas."

At Governor Reagan's second inaugural in 1971 there was a disturbance as chanting demonstrators threw an orange in the direction of the official stand, but they failed to hit anyone.

Familiar faces at a "Californians for Reagan" dinner at the Coconut Grove in Hollywood. From left to right: John Wayne, Bob Hope, Governor Ronald Reagan, Dean Martin, and Frank Sinatra.

Governor and Mrs. Ronald Reagan greet GI's at the Saigon airport during a short stopover in Vietnam. Reagan was touring Asia as President Nixon's emissary in October 1971, and he brought President Nguyen Van Thieu a message from the president to the effect that there would be "no change in the course or policy of our nation" toward Vietnam.

Back home in Sacramento, the governor and son Ron, Jr., play touch football in their backyard.

Governor Reagan (left) in Oakland throws out the first ball in the third game of the 1972 World Series, while the Oakland Athletics' owner (right) leans back, laughing.

Governor Ronald Reagan and Acting President S. I. Hayakawa of San Francisco State at a joint press conference, after conferring on student disturbances. The plaque in the foreground displays words from a campaign speech by the governor.

Ronald expressed his love this way: "How do you describe coming into a warm room from out of the cold? Never waking up bored? The only thing wrong is, she's made a coward out of me. Whenever she's out of sight I'm worried about her."

As promised, Ronald Reagan became a reform governor. He took a hard line with student dissent on college campuses and instituted college tuition. He froze state hiring, reduced the deficit, and raised taxes. In his second term he introduced income tax rebates, reduced property taxes, and cut the welfare rolls while increasing payments to those who qualified. The state's economy prospered while he was in office.

After only two years in office Ronald Reagan became a "back door" candidate for president at the 1968 Republican convention as California's "favorite son," part of a plan by conservatives to give him national prominence in preparation for a later, serious go at the presidency. At the Republican convention in Miami on August 4, 1968, delegate Ivy Baker Priest, treasurer of California, nominated Ronald Reagan; the nomination was followed by a huge cascade of balloons dropping on the delegates, accompanied by a twenty-minute floor demonstration. As expected, Richard Nixon won the nomination on the first ballot; Ronald Reagan was appointed to move that the convention make the vote unanimous.

So far Ronald had a single victory under his political belt. Then in 1970 he ran for reelection as governor, this time against Jesse Unruh, the Democratic leader of the state legislature. Once more Ronald Reagan's opponent made the mistake of underestimating him, trying at one point to picket his house to force an on-camera confrontation, but nobody was home. Unruh chased

In frosty Moultonborough, in northern New Hampshire, Ronald Reagan opens his 1976 campaign for the Republican presidential nomination, riding in a horse-drawn sleigh.

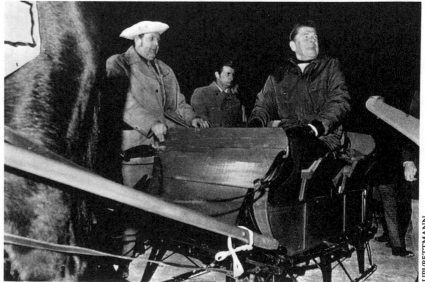

UPI/BETTMANN

Nancy Reagan pulls Ronald away from anti-Reagan pickets in Manchester, New Hampshire, during his campaign for the nomination. His opponent, President Gerald Ford, had just left after a vote-seeking visit to New Hampshire.

A tired trouper, Nancy Reagan catches a nap on her husband's lap after a swing through the South and East in search of delegates to the 1976 Republican National Convention.

the governor to the airport, but Reagan wasn't there either. Unruh looked foolish.

By now, Reagan was an even more polished performer, but his popularity had slipped since 1966. Although he won with 52 percent of the votes to Unruh's 47 percent, Unruh was gaining on him at the very end.

As 1974 arrived, his last year in office, everyone asked what next at age sixty-three for Ronald Reagan? Tentative plans to run for president after Nixon in 1976 were cancelled when Watergate brought on Gerald Ford for the two remaining years of Nixon's term.

Reagan left office with no intention of dropping out of the public eye. In 1974 he earned a whopping $800,000 writing a weekly syndicated news column, taping fifteen-minute commentaries for 350 radio stations daily, and travelling the lecture circuit at $5000 per appearance.

Then Ronald Reagan made what was probably the biggest blunder in his entire political career: He reversed his earlier decision not to run and decided to challenge President Gerald Ford, leader of his own party, for his place in the White House.

On November 20, 1975, Reagan announced his candidacy for president at the National Press Club in Washington, D.C. He delivered a speech claiming he was going to cut the annual federal outlay by $90 billion, balance the budget, and reduce taxes by 23 percent.

When the primaries began, Reagan, off to a bad start, lost the key states of New Hampshire and Florida to Ford. Even Illinois, his home state, deserted him, giving Ford a 60–40 victory. But then Reagan upset Ford in North Carolina by attacking him and Secretary of State Henry Kissinger on the issue of the Panama

A lovely young Reagan booster, sporting a funny hat, reflecting the enthusiasm of many young people at the Republican National Convention for the Reagan candidacy.

Candidate Reagan, with Nancy in foreground, gets a warm welcome in Kansas City. He told supporters he hoped to win the Republican nomination on the first ballot but that "it's easier on the second ballot."

With his vice-presidential running mate, Senator Richard Schweiker, a moderate who Reagan had hoped would draw middle-of-the-road delegate votes, the man from California steps forward to accept defeat at the hands of President Gerald Ford.

Canal, which was being returned to the Panamanians. He sounded as fired up as in the days when he gave his old GE speech. "We bought it, we paid for it, it's ours and we're going to keep it," he declared. Reagan swept Texas, Indiana, Alabama, and Georgia, pulling ahead in the delegate count. Then he lost badly in Michigan, a state he needed.

The race was all over before he and Nancy entered the convention hall in Kansas City, but behind the scenes Reagan had forced the Ford team to write a more conservative platform in return for his appearance on the podium to show conservative unity for the president.

At the convention's close a weary Ronald and Nancy retreated to rest aboard a friend's yacht in Florida. Reagan slept fourteen hours a night for two days, napping in the afternoon and generally taking it easy, trying to recover his spirit. It seemed to most people that it was the end of the aging politician's career; he would be sixty-six on his next birthday.

Ronald Reagan, always a hard fighter and always a good loser, congratulates Gerald Ford on winning the Republican presidential nomination on August 19, 1976.

SYGMA

10

THE RACE FOR THE PRESIDENCY (1979–1980)

One of our most cherished American dreams is the idea that any citizen can become president of the United States. The time had come for Ronald Wilson Reagan to try for the third time to realize that dream—to become the fortieth citizen elected president since 1789. His supporters knew Ronald Reagan's try for the presidency in 1980 at age sixty-nine was going to be his last.

The first primary was in Iowa. There Reagan went up against congressmen Philip Crane and John Anderson, senators Bob Dole and Howard Baker, ex-Governor John Connally, and George Bush. Polls showed Reagan in the lead.

He followed his advisers' plan, avoiding debates, holding himself aloof, although his instincts told him to join in. But he took campaign tactician John Sears' advice (Sears was a proponent of the "above the battle strategy"). Everyone was feeling confident. All Ronald Reagan had to do was sit tight and ride in on the popularity train.

Meanwhile George Bush, running hard, was working steadily day and night, making twice the appearances that Reagan made in Iowa.

On primary day, Reagan was in Beverly Hills, watching a screening of *Kramer vs. Kramer* in the home of producer Hal Wallis. Aides brought him the results after the screening. He had lost to Bush by 3 percent of the vote.

It shocked, scared, and angered him. "There are going to be some changes," he said firmly.

The New Hampshire primary was next, and Reagan decided to work much harder. He travelled by bus all over the state, making speeches for twenty-one days straight, including weekends. The exhausted press bus reporters who travelled with him put up a sign reading, "Free the Reagan 44."

A two-man debate had been arranged for Ronald Reagan and George Bush in Nashua. Reagan wanted the public encounter in order to cut Bush down to size, believing it would show up Bush as the weaker candidate. Bush wanted the debate so he could show it was a two-man race.

The Nashua *Telegraph* was to sponsor the debate, but Robert Dole complained that that constituted an unauthorized contribution to the two candidates' campaign. To get around that objection Reagan and Bush could split the costs, but Bush's campaign committee refused, leaving Reagan's team to pick up the entire bill.

Shortly before the night of the debate, polls revealed that Reagan had a solid lead, that he didn't need to meet Bush alone. John Sears quietly invited Crane, Dole, Anderson, and Baker to the debate. (John Connally was out of town, campaigning in the South.)

Ronald arrived at the Nashua school gymnasium. When Bush learned the others were present, he objected, claiming it violated the agreed-upon rules.

By now Reagan had decided he would not debate if the others were excluded. But that would mean he was walking out, conceding the night to Bush. Instead, taking the four forbidden candidates with him, he walked out on the stage and sat down, an angry look on his face. Bush, already in his seat, stared straight ahead. After a moment of awkward silence Reagan started to explain why it would be unfair not to hear all the candidates.

"Turn Mr. Reagan's microphone off!" commanded John Breen, editor of the *Telegraph*.

"I paid for this microphone, Mr. Green!" objected Reagan, getting the name wrong but the argument right as far as the audience was concerned. They wanted all six men to debate.

Reagan's righteous anger was effective. A stagehand brought out chairs for the four other candidates.

Reagan won the New Hampshire primary, handily beating Bush 51 percent to 27 percent.

In Florida Nancy campaigned with Ronald. It was becoming clear to the national media that Nancy Reagan might well be America's next First Lady.

In the end, Ronald Reagan won in twenty-nine primaries, Bush in only four. The others lost in every primary.

Ronald and Nancy Reagan arrive at the campus of the University of New Hampshire in February 1980, at the beginning of Reagan's quest for the presidential nomination. By this time, the New England snow was familiar.

Reagan's nomination was assured. He arrived in Detroit on Monday, July 16, six days before the convention.

"Nancy and I were just flying by and thought we'd drop in and see what's going on," he joked. Maureen, Michael, Patti, and Ron, Jr., joined their father's week of triumph.

In his acceptance speech Reagan talked about reducing inflation, making tax cuts, putting people back to work, cutting down the burdensome federal bureaucracy, and reversing the decline of American strength. The positive forces he extolled were family, neighborhood, work, peace, and freedom. He took his audience back to the beginning of the American experiment, reminding them of the heroes in American history from Lincoln to Franklin Roosevelt.

At the end he confessed, "I've been a little afraid to suggest what I'm going to say. I'm more afraid not to. Can we begin our crusade joined together in a moment of silent prayer?"

People stood up all over the arena and bowed their heads. He closed his speech, saying, "God bless America."

Ronald Reagan (left) and George Bush (right) with the moderator at the famous debate sponsored by the **Nashua Telegraph.** *The four other candidates for the presidential nomination had not yet appeared, but when they did, a near-riot ensued, with Reagan a clear winner over Bush in both the dispute and the debate that followed.*

In Springfield, Missouri, riding in a horse-drawn wagon driven by a man from the Ozarks, Reagan attends a down-home rally where his homspun style wins a lot of friends.

UPI/BETTMANN

Ronald Reagan campaigning in Florida, where he won another victory over George Bush in the primary campaign. Bush put up a hard fight in the primaries, while Reagan at first was lackadaisical. But after losing a few midwestern primaries, "the Gipper" built up a head of steam.

SYGMA

The campaign began with President Carter in trouble with the voters. He had all the advantages of an incumbent president, but the public was tired of the president's style. Inflation was rampant. With fifty two Americans held hostage in Iran, there was a feeling of national helplessness. The American people were ready for Ronald Reagan's optimism and his promise to return America to the days of small government and unfettered opportunity.

The decisive campaign event would be the October 28 television debate, a scant eight days before the election. At the time, polls showed Ronald in the lead by a narrow 6.62 percentage points.

In the debate, Carter made a major error while discussing nuclear war. "I had a discussion with my daughter, Amy, the other day," he said, "before I came here, to ask her what the most important issue was. She said she thought nuclear weaponry and the control of nuclear arms." His statement had the air of pandering to the audience. Why give a twelve-year-old's opinion on the world's most important problem when one is surrounded by a host of knowledgable experts? It was much less than the public expected of a president.

The second mishap came when Carter accused Reagan of campaigning against Medicare and then launched into a strong defense of the program.

"There you go again," Ronald Reagan replied regretfully, as if he had constantly to admonish this poor guy who just never could get the story straight. Carter's debating point was valid, but Reagan's casual remark made Carter look foolish and won the day.

99

In Detroit, Michigan, at the Republican nominating convention in July 1980, Nancy Reagan and Elizabeth Taylor applaud a speaker. Miss Taylor's then-husband, Senator John Warner of Virginia, addressed the group that was to nominate Nancy's husband, Ronald Reagan, for president.

UPI/BETTMANN

Republican vice-presidential candidate George Bush and former President Gerald Ford raise the arms of GOP standard-bearer Ronald Reagan after the acceptance speeches to the Republican National Convention on July 17, 1980, in Detroit.

UPI/BETTMANN

UPI/BETTMANN

Cozily together, Ronald and Nancy Reagan try out a rocking chair presented to them at the Neshoba County Fair in Philadelphia, Mississippi.

Republican presidential candidate Reagan launches his campaign against Jimmy Carter with an auspicious backdrop, the Statue of Liberty.

UPI/BETTMANN

The Reagan campaign entourage arrived in Michigan accompanied by former President Ford, finding crowds such as this holding strongly pro-Reagan views.

Ronald Reagan aboard the presidential campaign plane, which displayed a campaign poster humorously borrowing from one of his movies.

On the presidential trail in Detroit, Reagan met with officials from Ford, General Motors, and Chrysler, and, here, with assembly line workers.

Candidate Reagan consults with the Reverend Jesse Jackson on issues involving the black community and other minority voters.

The presidential hopeful, originally from Illinois, greets the bust of an illustrious predecessor in Springfield, Illinois. Tradition has it that rubbing the nose of the sculpture, outside Lincoln's tomb, will bring good luck.

Ronald Reagan, wearing a yarmulke, meets with members of a synagogue in Claremont, California.

A major issue of the presidential contest between Ronald Reagan and President Carter was Carter's failure to gain release of the fifty-two American hostages held in Iran.

Nancy and Ronald Reagan in their suite in Los Angeles' Century Plaza Hotel, watching the results roll in. A landslide!

President Carter (left) and Ronald Reagan (right) in the midst of their famous debate; Reagan turned the tide with "There you go again."

A stately setting: the United States Capitol, prepared for the inauguration of Ronald Wilson Reagan, fortieth president of the republic, on January 20, 1981.

Ronald Reagan is sworn in as president by Chief Justice Warren Burger. Nancy Reagan holds the Bible, as Senator Mark Hatfield (center) and former President Jimmy Carter (extreme right) look on.

The official Reagan family portrait was released by the White House shortly after the Inauguration. Shown with President Reagan and the First Lady (front, center) are: (left to right, standing, back row) Geoffrey Davis, Dennis Revell, Michael Reagan, Cameron Reagan (grandson of the President), Neil Reagan, Dr. Richard Davis, Ronald P. Reagan; (left to right, seated) Anne Davis, Maureen Reagan, Colleen Reagan, Bess Reagan, Patricia Davis, Patti Davis, and Doria Reagan.

Having become the nation's First Family earlier in the day, the president and First Lady leave the White House en route to a round of balls celebrating the Inauguration.

Nancy and Ronald Reagan break into laughter at the mimicry of comedian Rich Little (no doubt a presidential imitation) at the Inaugural gala honoring the newly installed president and First Lady.

Jimmy Carter had no chance to regain the lead after the debate. A majority felt that Ronald Reagan had won the confrontation.

On Election Day, Nancy and Ronald, at home in the late California afternoon, stood in front of the television screen when CBS commentators came on the air at 5:15 P.M. predicting a landslide win by over 8 million votes. The house quickly filled with friends, relatives, neighbors, working staff, and well-wishers.

"I'll bet there's a hot time in Dixon tonight," said Neil "Moon" Reagan, raising his voice above the din.

"I'd like to be there off in a corner just listening," said the president-elect of the United States, whose heart had never left his hometown.

It was Inauguration Day, January 20, 1981. Spectators stood ten deep along Pennsylvania Avenue, waiting to catch a glimpse of the president-elect. As Ronald Reagan rode slowly by in his open limousine with Nancy at his side, the crowd cheered and pressed forward against the barriers to get a closer look at the man who was riding in on a national tide of hope.

The Reagan inaugural speech expressed Ronald Reagan's life theme: the need to find strength in ourselves, to reach with courage for the American dream.

"Those who say we are in a time when there are no heroes— they just don't know where to look. You can see heroes every day, going in and out of factory gates. . . . You meet heroes across the counter—and they are on both sides of the counter. . . . I'm addressing the heroes of whom I speak—you, the citizens of this blessed land. Your dreams, your hopes, your goals are going to be the dreams, the hopes, and goals of this administration, so help me God. . . . Well, I believe we Americans of today are ready to act worthy of ourselves, ready to do what must be done to insure happiness and liberty for ourselves, our children, and our children's children. . . ."

Said a lady from West Virginia afterwards, "Oh, it was so good it made me cry." It was like a Ronald Reagan movie to her. "I can't believe how everything is coming out with a happy ending."

A happy aftermath to all the festivities was a ceremony welcoming back the newly released Iranian hostages. Here the president gives a flag to ex-hostage Bruce Laingen; an American flag was given by Reagan to each of the fifty-two just-released Americans.

UPI/BETTMANN

11

THE ASSASSINATION ATTEMPT (1981)

*I*t was the first day of Ronald Reagan's tenth week in office, Monday, March 31, 1981. Except for a short trip to the Washington Hilton to make an important speech to an AFL-CIO convention, he was scheduled to work all day in the Oval Office.

At noon he ate lunch alone upstairs in his private quarters, then he lay down to take a short nap. Nancy had to miss their daily lunch together, instead dining with cabinet wives in Georgetown at the home of Michael Ainslie, president of the National Trust for Historic Preservation.

Arriving at the Hilton at 2:00 P.M., the president was greeted by a small group of waiting reporters, photographers, and sightseers, held back by the Washington police. In the group on the sidewalk was John Hinckley, Jr., carrying a gun in his pocket.

Ronald made a ten-minute speech in the banquet room to 3500 leaders of the Building and Construction Trades Department of the AFL-CIO and then left.

Hinckley, waiting outside to kill the president, probably had the most singular reason of any assassin who ever tried to shoot an American president. All the others had wanted revenge, believing the president had in some way abused them, but Hinckley held no grievance against Ronald Reagan. He wanted to kill the president to show movie actress Jody Foster how far he would go to get her attention and thus prove his love. (Hinckley was obsessed with Miss Foster, who had never met him and had no connection with him.)

At 2:24 P.M., Ronald Reagan, coming out of the double doors of the Hilton, walked to his limousine and stopped, raising his left arm to greet the cheering people in the building across the street.

Hinckley pulled his gun and fired six shots in quick succession, hitting Secret Service agent Timothy J. McCarthy, Washington policeman Thomas K. Delahanty, Press Secretary James Brady, and President Ronald Reagan.

Luckily, the Reagan bullet, a .22 Devastator designed to break up into small fragments and tear up the insides of the body, struck the armored rear panel of the limousine first. The bullet flattened out like a serrated coin, cancelling the explosive element, then passed between the car and the open rear door and hit the president in the left chest under his upraised arm.

At the sound of shots, Jerry Parr, head of the Secret Service detail, pushed the president down and inside the car. The president hit his head on the edge of the car, falling face-down across the bulge of the carpeted transmission. Parr, moving swiftly, threw himself down on top of the president. "Take off," he shouted at the driver. "Just take off."

Ronald felt a sharp stab of pain. "You broke my ribs," he cried out, lying under Parr as the car sped off. He did not think he had been shot, nor did Parr.

The Secret Service agent immediately ran his hands over the president's body—along his chest, back, and under his arms—and found nothing.

Parr went on the radio. "Rawhide not hurt, repeat, not hurt," he said, using the president's code name.

Suddenly Reagan coughed. Blood came to his lips. The deep red color told Parr it had come from the lungs, the result, he assumed, of rib damage from the fall to the floor. Parr ordered the driver to go to the George Washington Hospital.

At the assassination scene there was chaos. The three other wounded men were rushed by ambulance to the George Washington Hospital. The police and Secret Service had Hinckley pinned to the ground. They wrenched the gun out of his hand, then rushed him away in handcuffs, blocking him on all sides to make certain he would reach jail alive.

At the hospital, Reagan, walking white-faced and in pain through the doors of the George Washington emergency entrance, started to collapse. A nurse and a paramedic grabbed him before he could fall, rushed him to the trauma room, and laid him on a work table.

Three nurses, working on the president simultaneously, cut off his shirt and suit, throwing them on the floor. They made an incision in his chest and inserted a tube to draw off the blood

President Ronald Reagan leaves the Washington Hilton at about 2:15 P.M. on March 31, 1981, after a ten-minute speech to 3500 members of the Building and Construction Trades Department of the AFL-CIO, and waves to the crowd outside the hotel, moments before he is shot. From left are Secret Service Agent Jerry Parr (in raincoat), who shoved Reagan into the limousine; Press Secretary James Brady, who was seriously wounded; Reagan; Michael Deaver, Reagan's aide; an unidentified policeman; Washington policeman Thomas K. Delahanty, who was shot; and Secret Service Agent Timothy J. McCarthy, who was also shot.

President Reagan waves and then looks up as he is shot, before being shoved into the presidential limousine by Agent Jerry Parr (right in bottom photo), who still didn't realize that Reagan had been hit.

Chaos reigns right after the shooting, as one agent pushes the president's limousine and others search for the assailant.

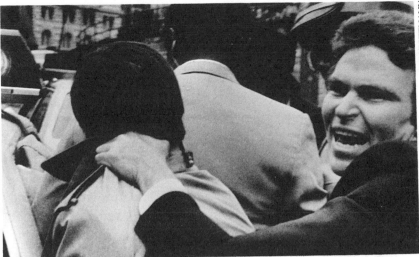

Confusion and panic are written on the face of one witness to the assassination attempt.

Agents rush to surround the would-be assassin, as one victim, Secret Service Agent McCarthy lies helpless on the sidewalk.

Agent McCarthy (foreground) and Washington policeman Delahanty (center) still lie on the ground, as aides minister to Presidential Press Secretary Brady (rear).

The same scene moments later, as Secret Service men surround the assailant, who is later identified as John Hinckley, Jr.

111

that was filling up his left pleural cavity to clear it so they could take X rays to locate the bullet.

Nancy Reagan, arriving back at the White House, was told there had been a shooting at the hotel, that the president was not hurt but was now at George Washington Hospital. When she arrived at the hospital, Mike Deaver, deputy chief of staff, said, "He's taken a bullet, but he's all right."

Nancy wanted to see him at once, but the medical team said no, they needed time to clean up the trauma room. They knew how devastating it would be for a wife to walk into a trauma room and find her husband lying in surroundings with blood spattered everywhere. While she waited, attendants picked the president's clothes up from the floor, and cleaned away the spattered blood and discarded swabs.

Nancy Reagan walked into the room and grew pale, but she did not lose her composure. She put her hand in her husband's and leaned forward to kiss him on the forehead.

"Honey, I forgot to duck," he said.

Dr. Daniel Ruge, the White House physician, and Dr. Benjamin Aaron, head of Cardiothoracic Surgery at George Washington Hospital, agreed that they should start the search for the bullet immediately because Reagan was still bleeding and they were afraid he would go into shock.

Nancy Reagan, accompanied by a Secret Service agent, arriving at George Washington University Hospital, carrying a jar of jelly-beans for the president, who is recovering from surgery.

A week after the assassination attempt a special photo was taken by the White House photographer and released nationally showing the president on his feet. The picture was meant to reassure an anxious public that he was on his way to recovery.

The convalescent Ronald Reagan, still in the hospital, looks at a giant get-well card showing all the members of the White House staff.

They got Nancy's consent to operate and immediately rolled him into the operating room, followed by a band of medical personnel and Secret Service men.

Ronald looked around and quipped, "I hope you're all Republicans." They assured him they were all Republicans that day, then put him under anesthesia.

Dr. Aaron opened up Reagan's chest and explored the area around his heart. There was no critical damage, but the bullet had only just missed the aorta and heart. He followed the bullet's track down to the seventh rib and then upward into the lung. He couldn't find the bullet, though he knew it had to be somewhere nearby. He pushed a catheter into the bullet's track and followed with his finger, pressing the area around the catheter. At last, he said aloud that he thought he had it; he got a finger on it and pulled it downward and out. That was the only operation the president would need.

When Reagan's breathing tube was removed upon recovery from the surgery and he was switched to an oxygen mask, he was given a pad and pencil so he could write what he wanted to say. He asked about the others who had been wounded and was appalled by the news, feeling responsible, that they had been hurt because of him. He also asked about Hinckley, but no one as yet had the answer as to why the young man had attempted the assassination.

Thousands of get-well letters, telegrams, and gifts poured into the White House and the hospital. These were taken across the street from the White House to be opened in a special mailroom first as a safety precaution.

Everyone wanted reassurance that the president was actually recovering as speedily as the press releases said he was. The White House took a picture of Reagan in bed and Nancy leaning

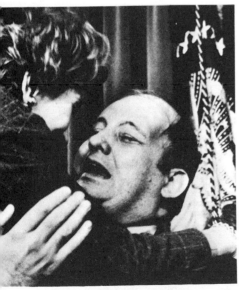

The First Lady hugs White House Press Secretary James Brady, still in a wheelchair and speech-impaired after the shooting, at the opening of the refurbished White House press center.

The face of would-be assassin John Warnock Hinckley, Jr., in a 1981 Colorado Highway Department photo. His motives were the strangest of all who have made attempts on the lives of American presidents.

over kissing him, cropping out all signs of medical equipment. On April 12, thirteen days after he had entered George Washington, Ronald Reagan left the hospital with the working staff gathered together to bid him good-bye and good luck.

His wit and spirit and his Hollywood stories and jokes had made the staff delight in his company. David Broder of the *Washington Post* wrote, "When he displayed that same wit and grace in the hours after his own life was threatened, he elevated those appealing human qualities to the level of legend."

Slowly his old ebullience, alertness, and strength returned, and he was back riding horses at the ranch and cutting brush. The nation's doubts that at seventy he might be too old to take a terrible wound and would not really recover were dissipated when they saw him looking vital once more. What amazed everyone was that Ronald Wilson Reagan could come out of this near-tragedy laughing and telling jokes. His popularity rose higher than ever, even among those who disagreed with his politics. As Democrat Tip O'Neill, Speaker of the House, once put it, "There's just something about the guy that people like. They want him to be a success."

Later, during a press interview evaluating his first six months in office, the president was asked if there was anything he'd done that he would have changed. He replied, "I wouldn't have gone to the Hilton."

President Ronald Reagan is welcomed back to the White House by a banner and a large group of admiring staffers after his release from the hospital.

114

12
CHINA AND IRELAND
(1984)

*I*n China, a land where the elderly are highly respected, Ronald Reagan, at age seventy-three, was regarded with a reverence that made him slightly uncomfortable. He'd spent most of his political life convincing people he'd found the Fountain of Youth. But the Chinese and Americans did have a common admiration for his vigor at age seventy-three.

"After such a long flight, you don't look tired at all," said Prime Minister Zhao Ziyang, sixty-four, complimenting the president during the first meeting in the Great Hall of the People in Peking. "You look very energetic at your age. It's very rare."

Part of Reagan's secret was avoiding jet lag on the long trip from Santa Barbara to China by way of Honolulu and Guam by going on the "F" anti–jet lag diet (feast, fast, feast, fast) designed by Dr. Charles F. Ehret of the Department of Energy. Four days before leaving on April 22, 1984, he began the diet, which combines a high protein breakfast and lunch with a high carbohydrate dinner on the first and third days and dwindles to salad and fruit on alternate days. Coffee is permitted only at certain hours and no alcohol is permitted while flying. One aide thought the diet's strong attraction was the macaroni and cheese on feast days, which the president of the United States loves dearly.

"Well, thank you very much," Reagan replied with a smile.

"People here say you look much younger than your age," added the prime minister through an interpreter.

"As far as I'm concerned," said Ronald, who had come six thousand miles to do international horse trading, "the meeting has already been a success."

At a formal state dinner in a giant room at the Great Hall, President Reagan was given two colored steel balls to roll in the palms of his hands to prevent arthritis.

Reagan followed up on his host's interest in his age, declaring that in America people also revere their elders. Then he made a dramatic observation, one he'd probably never make at home. "My own lifetime spans one-third of the history of the American republic."

Ronald Reagan had come to China to make friends, open new markets for American trade, and establish a foundation for opposing the Soviet Union's expansionist foreign policy. "We journey to China in a spirit of peace and friendship, realistic about our differences but desiring to build upon our common interests."

These were remarkable words, coming as they did from a man who had spent much of his prepresidential political life denouncing the government in Peking as illegitimate. He had moved to Carter's position of loosening ties to Taiwan and recognizing Peking as the legitimate government of mainland China. What Ronald Reagan liked about China was that vast nation's ability to keep fifty Russian divisions occupied on the Chinese-Soviet border—not to mention the $12 billion in foreign trade with China.

China was anxious to buy nuclear reactor equipment that the United States wanted to sell, with the proviso that China would not enrich or reprocess fuel or store materials to be used for making nuclear arms.

The country most concerned about the Reagan trip was Taiwan, which feared America would put pressure on the island nation to compromise its independence of Red China. But

President Reagan on what he has called his most significant foreign mission, has lunch with Chinese leader Deng Xiaoping in Peking on April 28, 1984, after their morning talks.

The Reagans, flanked by Chinese officials, explore the Great Wall of China, said to be the only man-made structure visible from outer space.

Reagan had assured the Taiwanese prior to the meeting with China's leaders that the United States would not set a date for ending arms sales to Taiwan, would not play mediator between Taipei and Peking, would not revise the Taiwan Relations Act, and would not pressure Taiwan to enter into negotiations with Peking.

Reagan and Zhao got into an argument over the Soviet Union. Indeed, Reagan made two speeches over Chinese television that were cut off the air whenever, without naming the Soviets, he touched on expansionist policies of foreign governments. The underlying reason was that China and the Soviet Union were having talks about normalizing relations after twenty-five years of border clashes, and the Chinese did not want Reagan upsetting the applecart. China and the United States both wanted a reduction of missiles and Soviet troop strength along China's northern frontier, withdrawal of Soviet forces from Afghanistan, and an end to Soviet support of Vietnam's occupation of Cambodia. China opposed the American position on Nicaragua. China thought the United States should open talks with the Palestine Liberation Organization, which the president turned down out of hand. The president suggested that China could be of help in uniting the two Koreas, but Zhao wanted no part of dealing with North Korea. China also wanted the United States to reduce the sale of arms to Taiwan, which the president declined to do.

The president and the prime minister did sign a three-part pact. The agreement limited China's tax on American corporations doing business in China, defined areas of nuclear cooperation, and expanded cultural exchanges to include artists, journalists, writers, sports teams, and dance and stage performers.

Nancy Reagan, a great hit on the trip to China, helps feed a bottle of milk to a baby panda at the Peking Zoo. Mrs. Reagan brought a "Pennies for Pandas" check from American schoolchildren, which was donated to the Chinese people.

The First Lady dances with Liu Yu, age six, at a neighborhood school in Peking. The Reagans believed their Chinese journey opened up many doors.

WIDE WORLD

The feasts were fabulous. The banquet room of the Great Hall of the People, a vast ivory and gold-columned room, glowed under dozens of scalloped and petal-shaped light fixtures at a nine-course dinner honoring President and Mrs. Reagan, given by China's Prime Minister Zhao Ziyang. The guests were awestruck by the quantity and variety of Oriental food. At the head table, the first-course dishes alone included asparagus, chicken, pork, noodles, beans, shrimp, peanuts, and cheese, all arrayed on small plates around the perimeter.

The next day the Reagans invited their hosts to a dinner billed as completely American, based on a traditional Thanksgiving feast, featuring turkey flown in from the United States. Embassy staff and the White House advance group had been planning the dinner for several weeks. The final results, however, as one senior White House official admitted, tasted like a frozen TV dinner.

Nancy made a bigger hit than the turkey. Deng Xiaoping asked her to return some day without her husband. Lin Jiamel, the wife of President Li Xianian, took her to visit a typical school, where the children called her "auntie" because they said she was too young to be a grandmother.

The Reagans were awestruck by the Great Wall of China and the 2000-year-old tomb of Emperor Shih Huang Ti at Xi'ah, one of the eight wonders of the world, containing an army of life-sized terra cotta figures of soldiers and horses. Some 800 of an estimated 8000 buried for centuries had been excavated thus far.

Near the end of the trip, when Ronald Reagan and party reached Shanghai, he was amazed to find hundreds of thousands of Chinese jamming the streets to see him as hc completed the last of his six days in China. He had never experienced a crowd so large. Enthusiastic applause burst from students at Fudan University when he spoke of America's plans to help China develop skills in science and management techniques. "My trip to China," he told them, "has been as important and enlightening as any I've ever taken as president. I see America and our Pacific neighbors going forward in a mighty enterprise to build strong economies and a safer world. The United States and China have an historic opportunity. We can expand economic and scientific cooperation, strengthen the ties between our peoples, and take an important step toward peace and a better life."

Attending a London economic conference in June of 1984, the President and Nancy took a side trip first to Ballyporeen, Ireland, where his great great grandfather, Michael Reagan was born and eventually emigrated to America in 1858 after the Great Potato Famine. Only recently had Ronald Reagan learned his roots were

At O'Farrell's Pub in Ballyporeen, Ireland, the village that was the Reagan ancestral home, Ronald Reagan and Nancy Reagan toast one another in the native brew.

The president and First Lady (extreme right) watch Irish folk dancers in Ballyporeen.

The president jokes with his audience about receiving Bally-poreen's highest honor. The town pub was renamed Ronald Reagan in his honor.

In Ireland, on a side trip without Ronald, who was busy visiting Parliament, Nancy attends the unveiling of a portrait at the Royal College of Surgeons in Dublin honoring her internationally famous stepfather, Dr. Loyal Davis.

President Ronald Reagan is served a farewell glass of ale in a typical Irish public house.

in Ballyporeen, after interested genealogists began tracing the President's family history in old church, marriage and tax records.

Walking slowly through the streets of the tiny village, amid the bright green hills of Tipperary County, Ronald and Nancy stopped first in a moment of high drama and emotion to worship at the modest old stone Church of the Assumption where his great great grandfather had been baptized.

After a visit to John O'Farrell's pub in the center of town, renamed The Ronald Reagan, he told a crowd of three thousand well wishers standing in a drizzling rain, "Thanks to you good people who have dug into the history of a poor immigrant family I know at last whence I came. And this has given my soul a new contentment. And it is a joyous feeling. It is like coming home after a long journey. Today I come back to you as a descendant of people who are buried here in pauper graves. Perhaps this is God's way of reminding us that we must always treat every individual no matter what his or her station in life with dignity and respect."

Queen Elizabeth of England, at a state dinner in San Francisco in 1983, deadpans a crack about California weather and breaks up President Reagan.

UPI/BETTMANN

13
CAMPAIGN
AND REELECTION
(1984)

*T*he 1984 presidential campaign resembled the 1980 campaign in one important respect: The two planned debates between Ronald Reagan and Walter "Fritz" Mondale, vice-president in the Carter administration, could make or break either candidate, even though this time Ronald Reagan was leading his opponent at the outset by a 20-point margin.

There was one difference in that the second-banana debate between Vice President George Bush and Democratic candidate Geraldine Ferraro had aroused unusual interest. Ferraro came off very well, equal to Bush, which was the same as a win for the underdog. Bush made the error of patronizing Ferraro, which had a backlash effect.

Ronald Reagan's performance in the main event, the first Reagan-Mondale debate, held in Louisville at the Kentucky Center, was a fiasco. No doubt it will be recorded as the low point in his twenty-year career in politics. He was at a loss for words, often groping for numbers, struggling and stumbling to keep his syntax and thoughts in order, and showing every one of his seventy-three years. Offstage, the Reagan people could hear the Mondale people cheering in their dressing room.

"It's going to bring up the age issue," said Dick Wirthlin, Reagan's private pollster. What had gone wrong with the president's thinking and his rehearsals for the debate? Something was

A potent poster designed for the 1984 Reagan-Bush reelection campaign, with all the winning ingredients: the president, the vice-president, the White House and, of course, the flag as a background.

First Lady Nancy Reagan, after delivering a speech to the Republican National Convention on August 22, 1984, turns to wave to the president, whose image is projected on the large screen behind the podium. Reagan was watching the proceedings from his hotel suite.

UPI/BETTMANN

The grand finale of the Dallas convention included a barrage of balloons. The president and Nancy Reagan and the vice-president and Mrs. Bush wave to the faithful from the podium.

Vice President George Bush wipes his brow as he debates Democratic vice-presidential candidate Geraldine Ferraro in Philadelphia on October 11, 1984. Moderator Sander Vanocur is seated between them. Some said Bush came out second best to Ferraro, the first woman to be nominated for vice-president by a major political party.

not right. The campaign team had sensed that Reagan was at a distance when boning up for the debate, preparing for it without spirit, like college exams he had crammed for by looking at the books for one hour on the night before the test. He got C's then, which was all he wanted in college, but he needed an A in campaigning.

For all Reagan's slippage in the first debate, he was still ahead until he came to his closing statement. He asked his key question: Were Americans better off than four years before? Then, instead of driving to a grand finale ("Give me a chance to finish the job that we together have begun."), he lost the thread of his thought and wandered into a detailed, boring list of his accomplishments in office.

Nancy was angry, feeling White House aides had brutalized Ronald. The press jumped in with their speculation, and the issue became not what was said at the debate, but whether the president was growing senile. Dr. Ruge, the White House physician, was cornered by the press and asked if Reagan had lost stamina over the last four years. Ruge said, in effect, that they'd have to ask the president.

The doctor's indiscretion created a surge of alarm in the Reagan camp. Jim Baker rushed out copies of the president's latest medical report, affirming him to be a mentally alert, robust man who looked younger than his seventy-three years.

Debate II strategy was to keep Reagan wrapped in the flag

The main event was the second debate between President Reagan and Democratic challenger Walter Mondale. Although polls showed that Reagan had fumbled away the first debate, he won handily in the second confrontation in Kansas City on October 21, 1984. Edwin Newman (in the foreground) *is the moderator.*

until November voting time, to get him back to his tried-and-true styles and his trust in his own instincts—in short, to let Reagan be Reagan, which is what he does best. They got out Harry Truman's old steam train for a one-day whistle-stop campaign tour of Ohio. It was a gloves-off, give-'em-hell-Harry day, a tonic for Reagan that returned him to his old fighting stance, bristling again with total confidence.

The Mondale strategy was to hurt Reagan by focusing on his age, his allegedly inadequate knowledge of government affairs, and his incomplete grasp of issues. Pity, disdain, and ridicule were all potentially useful. Don't attack the president personally, but expose his weaknesses as a leader. Show that he's out of touch, that he doesn't understand the world, that he's in no position to be commander-in-chief.

Reagan's rehearsals for the second debate used a more informal group of coaches, old friends debating in a casual atmosphere, sitting together on a couch in his private quarters. The result was a much stronger command of the answers to tough questions.

As he took the elevator down to the debate, the president was warned that a reporter might ask him questions about his age. "I can handle that," said Reagan emphatically, without explaining how he was going to do it.

Nancy sat in the front row, where Ronald could see her. To lighten the mood, Jim Baker had had cue cards prepared, reading, "Have a good time" and "Chuckle."

As the debate began, a startling reversal was evident. This time it was Mondale who looked older on stage, with bags under his eyes and features sagging. Mondale attempted to take charge of the debate, but that didn't work. His charges of mistakes and errors by Reagan did not stick because the president coolly denied them. When Mondale questioned him about his age, the older man was ready. "I want you to know that I will not make age an issue of this campaign. I am not going to exploit for political purposes my opponent's youth and inexperience." Even Mondale had to laugh as the president buried the age issue forever—and won the debate.

Mondale's campaign may be best remembered for his having chosen the first woman vice-presidential candidate and for asking, "Where's the beef?"

Reagan's romantic vision of America and its dreams once again returned him to the presidency in his last campaign for public office. He won forty-nine of the fifty states, all except Mondale's home state of Minnesota and the District of Columbia; the popular vote was 54 million to 37 million—59 percent to 41 percent. It was also clearly Ronald Reagan's last hurrah.

When Ronald Reagan took the oath of office for his second term as president, he used The New Indexed Bible, *King James version, shown here. It belonged to his mother, Nelle Reagan.*

UPI/BETTMANN

Nancy Reagan holds the president's mother's Bible as her husband is sworn in by Chief Justice Warren Burger on January 21, 1985.

UPI/BETTMANN

President Reagan shakes the trunk and pats the head of an eighteen-month-old Asiatic female elephant named Jayathu, presented by President Jayewardene of Sri Lanka during a state visit. The elephant was given to the National Zoo in Washington.

WIDE WORLD

President Reagan and the First Lady are photographed at the wedding of daughter Patti Davis *(third from right) and her bride-groom, Paul Grilley, in Los Angeles. The groom's parents, Terrance F. Grilley and Donna Grilley, of Columbia Falls, Montana, are at the left.*

Reagan blows a whistle to start the Ringling Brothers and Barnum and Bailey Circus in Washington, with the help of the regular ringmaster. The president on this occasion launched a new "safe kids" program for missing children.

At the annual live Thanksgiving turkey presentation at the White House, Ronald Reagan ducks the flying feathers of a fifty-three-pound bird named "R.J." (for "robust and juicy").

129

The First Lady and the president, flanked by Jacqueline Kennedy Onassis and Senator Edward Kennedy, at a fund-raising event for the John F. Kennedy Memorial Library on June 24, 1985.

Mstislav Rostropovich, distinguished musician and director of the National Symphony Orchestra, delivers a kiss for the president while Nancy Reagan looks on approvingly. The occasion was a state dinner in honor of Indian Prime Minister Rajiv Gandhi.

WIDE WORLD

Returning to the New York stage for a one-night performance, Nancy Reagan is among the famous guests honoring the venerable Mary Martin for her fifty years in show business. Mrs. Reagan, who in 1946 had a small part in Lute Song, *a Broadway musical that starred Mary Martin, sang one of the show's hit songs, "Mountain High, Valley Low," to the audience at the Shubert Theatre.*

Time out for a little horse play in the Oval Office as the president and Dan Lurie, editor of a physical fitness magazine, have a go at arm wrestling. The president, rightly honored as the "best physically fit president ever," apparently earned the title by winning the match.

The President's penchant for jellybeans brings him a big laugh when, at the end of a sumptuous political dinner in a Washington hotel, one of the guests hands the president his "dessert." Reagan's attraction for the candy started in his days as governor, when he used it as a substitute to help him break his smoking habit.

Nobel Laureate Mother Theresa offers the traditional Indian clasped-hands sign of thanks to the president and First Lady after receiving America's highest civilian award, the Medal of Freedom, for her inspiring work among the poor.

14

THE CANCER CRISIS
(1985)

he President has cancer."

Dr. Steven Rosenberg paused in his announcement as he stood on the stage of the crowded auditorium at the Bethesda Naval Hospital, aware of the import and shock of his words to the audience of media people. A low murmur passed through the hall as the press waited to hear more and to question Rosenberg, one of the six doctors who had operated on Ronald Reagan the previous day, removing a cancerous polyp from his colon. After spending two hours and fifty-three minutes removing eighteen inches of Ronald Reagan's large colon, the six-man surgical team had sent the polyp to the lab to determine whether the growth was benign or malignant, a test that took twenty-four hours.

Less than an hour before the operation, Vice President George Bush was handed a signed letter from President Reagan that said simply, "I have determined and it is my intention and direction that Vice President George Bush shall discharge presidential powers and duties in my stead, commencing with the administration of anesthesia to me."

On July 27, 1985, at 11:28 A.M., George Herbert Walker Bush became the first man ever designated acting president of the United States. He held the job for eight hours, until 7:22 P.M., when Reagan reclaimed his duties and powers.

It all started innocently enough on Friday, July 13, 1985, when Reagan took the morning off to go to the Bethesda Medical Center for routine removal of a noncancerous polyp found in March in the lower portion of his colon. A year earlier, in May 1984, he had had another small polyp removed.

This time the doctors decided to probe farther, using a colonoscope, a lengthy flexible tube with a fiber optic viewing device and a tool for snipping the thin stalks that usually join polyps to the colon wall. Moving the tube deeper, the surgeon found a growth on the president's cecum, the section of the colon near the small intestine, just above the appendix. The growth had obviously been there a long time, since it was too large to cut with the colonoscope, and it looked suspiciously like a malignancy called villous adenoma, with tentacles on its surface.

When Ronald Reagan went to Bethesda for this supposedly minor operation, the press took little interest, because the earlier surgery had been regarded as insignificant. At Larry Speakes' usual afternoon press conference in the White House, the reporters listened in surprised shock as Speakes announced that the doctors had found a precancerous polyp. The president had chosen to have surgery for its removal the next day rather than wait several weeks.

In the operating room, Captain Dale Oller, chief of surgery at Bethesda, opened the president's abdomen, removed eighteen inches of intestine, and looked around for further signs of cancer. He had fast pathological studies of tissue of the colon itself done. They turned out negative, and he sewed the chief executive up. The polyp itself was put in a container with a chemical solution and left for twenty-four hours. It was then sliced into microscopic sections, stained, and examined.

At 2:40 on Monday afternoon, the doctors arrived to speak with Nancy, who was seated in an L-shaped sitting room adjoining Ronald's bedroom. Her eyes filled with tears. "Oh, God," she sighed. The physicians told her they believed they had removed all of the cancerous growth. The cancer had not spread to the lymph nodes, and the likelihood of recurrence was less than 50 percent—even more remote in men Ronald Reagan's age.

Nancy wanted to be the one to tell Ronald. When she entered his room with the doctors, she found him reading a book on Calvin Coolidge. He listened quietly as she spoke, his only response being that he was glad they had removed it all and that he would leave all the details to Nancy. As for recuperation, when could he get back on a horse? The doctors promised he would be back riding in a month. The discussion was over in five minutes, and Reagan was back to Calvin Coolidge.

The discovery of the malignancy caused the doctors to be suspicious of the care the president had previously received. Why hadn't he been examined more thoroughly and the polyp discovered earlier? Why weren't more extensive tests performed in

First Lady Nancy Reagan greets her spouse, President Ronald Reagan, in his hospital bed at Bethesda Naval Hospital on July 14, 1985 the day after he underwent surgery for removal of a precancerous polyp in his intestine.

To cheer up the presidential patient, Nancy Reagan brings a large bunch of balloons on one of her many visits.

UPI/BETTMANN

On July 18, from the window of his hospital room, President Ronald Reagan gives the "A-OK" sign and is seconded by a wave from Nancy.

WIDE WORLD

WIDE WORLD

Well on his way to recovery one week after his cancer operation, the president waves to friends from the Truman balcony of the White House on the day of his return home from Bethesda Naval Hospital for two weeks of work and rest, to be followed by an extended vacation at Rancho del Cielo.

On August 1, fully recovered from surgery, the president explained that the scab on his nose was the result of the removal of a patch of skin diagnosed as basal cell carcinoma, an easily treated form of cancer usually caused by overexposure to the sun. The problem has not recurred.

WIDE WORLD

May 1984, after the first polyp was found? And why wasn't a more exhaustive examination made when a second polyp was discovered and Reagan was found to have blood in his stool? The president, for some inexplicable reason, hadn't had a physical examination in 1982 or in 1983. The White House medical staff found the first polyp when they finally gave him a physical exam in 1984. Dr. Ruge had decided the polyp wasn't something to worry about, although he'd secretly had it biopsied. In the course of the 1984 physical, only the lower portion of Reagan's colon was examined, so the doctors missed the big one, which was precancerous.

Earlier, in January 1985, two benign polyps had been found in the colon of Neil "Moon" Reagan, seventy-six. In view of the fact that family patterns are frequently observed in the development of such growths, that finding should have led to an examination of the president's entire colon in March 1985, but Neil Reagan's physicians did not inform the White House of their findings. Then cancer was discovered in Neil Reagan's colon in June 1985, a month before they found it in brother Ronald. (Neil Reagan had the same operation as the president, but five weeks later.)

Now it was Nancy Reagan's job to take over White House operations, with the help of Chief of Staff Donald Regan, who Nancy decided would be Ronald's only visitor during the period of recuperation. No phone calls were to be allowed, and if Vice

SYGMA

When the president was recovering from his operation, he went to the family ranch, Rancho del Cielo, a nearly 700-acre spread overlooking the ocean north of Los Angeles. In this and the following pictures, we see Ronald Reagan's favorite place for escape from the affairs of state.

The grounds are simply land-
scaped and include a large pool
in the rear of the house.

Ronald Reagan reintroduces
himself to two of his beloved
horses.

President Bush wanted to see the president, he had to clear it first through Regan and get Nancy's final okay. Later Nancy allowed morning briefings with national security adviser Robert Mc-Farlane, White House spokesman Larry Speakes, and Regan. For the next three weeks she allowed only one state visit—from China's President Li Xianian.

A month after his cancer operation, the president took a three-week vacation at Rancho del Cielo, the retreat he deeply loves, where through work, play, and isolation he renewed his energy, vigor, and spirit.

The presidential rancher still chops wood at Rancho del Cielo and resents being accused of doing it to show off.

The Reagans, with a helper, prepare to serve a traditional Thanksgiving dinner at the ranch.

According to a *Newsweek* poll, 57 percent of the public believed the president fit to resume a second term—unchanged from before Reagan's reelection. Furthermore, the *Newsweek* poll showed Reagan's job-approval rating had risen to 68 percent, his highest rating while in office.

Some observers think the most significant event of Ronald Reagan's first term was his surviving an assassin's bullet, not his tax cuts or legislative changes. And perhaps the most important event of his second term was his surviving cancer. In view of the feelings of vulnerability and helplessness Americans have felt in the face of such events, Reagan's resilience, strength, and good humor in the face of adversity account for his great popularity. He is perhaps the most popular president in American history.

Just a month after the operation, Ronald Reagan announced that a small basal cell carcinoma, a fairly common and easily curable form of skin cancer, had been surgically removed from his nose. The cancer was probably brought on by overexposure to the sun while horseback riding and cutting brush around the ranch, and it was treated by simple removal of the skin tissue.

The president at play, trying on one of his wide assortment of hats.

A rare photograph of the consummate actor off-guard, in one of his favorite chairs, talking relaxedly on the telephone.

*Reagan, with Nancy in the fore-
ground, surrounded by furnish-
ings in a low-key Western style.*

*The living room at Rancho del
Cielo is spacious, simple, and
above all comfortable.*

Ronald and Nancy fooling around in a hammock—a couple that never tires of each other's company.

15

REAGAN AT THE SUMMIT; THE GANDER AND *CHALLENGER* TRAGEDIES (1985–1986)

Millions were watching on television.

The two most powerful men in the world were about to meet on the steps of the Fleur d'Eau, a lakeside villa serving as the U.S. headquarters for the 1985 summit meeting. President Ronald Reagan, erect as a West Point cadet, waited just inside the villa's front door. It was a typically frigid, frosty winter day in Geneva, Switzerland, site of many earlier international conferences, home of many broken dreams of world peace.

"Okay," said an aide, receiving the electronic signal from the Secret Service agent on the front steps. "He's here." The aide opened the front door.

The president walked briskly down the steps and waited for Mikhail Gorbachev, a stocky, balding man twenty years his junior, approaching eagerly from his Ziv limousine.

Both men smiled warmly and shook hands as television cameras recorded for the millions watching what the world hoped would be the beginning of a new era of peace between the two superpowers.

The two men had come primarily to bargain on arms control. Ronald Reagan's controversial "star wars" antimissile defense program was a major issue. In the six years since the last summit meeting, suspicion and hostility between America and the Soviet Union had reached the most dangerous level since the coldest days of the Cold War.

On the first day, the president and the premier were scheduled for a fifteen-minute meeting, with numerous counselors present. Instead, by mutual agreement, they met privately for five hours, seated at a fireplace with only translators present.

Ronald Reagan offered his vision of a safer world. He asked Gorbachev to join him in his dream of rendering nuclear weapons obsolete with a space-based missile system.

Gorbachev replied, "It's an impractical dream. Who can control it? Who can monitor it? It opens up an arms race in space." The Soviet leader reasserted his country's peaceful intentions toward the United States and the world.

Reagan replied calmly, "As I said to you, I have a right to think you want to use your missiles against us. With mere words we cannot abolish the threat."

Frustrated, Gorbachev exclaimed, "Why don't you believe us when we say we will not use these weapons against you."

After some deliberation Ronald Reagan replied, "I cannot say to the American people that I can take you at your word if *you* don't believe *us*."

And thus the dialogue continued for five hours. Gorbachev found Reagan to be articulate, friendly, and well informed, willing to make concessions except on the U.S. missile defense system. Reagan discovered Mikhail Gorbachev to be smart, tough, and charming—and more flexible than expected.

Still, at the end of that first day, the two leaders remained at an impasse. They put on their coats and, joined by aides, went out the back door of the villa and took a walk down to the pool house.

For a while they walked in silence. Then Reagan said, "I think that we agree this meeting is useful."

"Yes," said Gorbachev.

"Then we must meet again," said the president, and he invited the Kremlin leader to come to America.

"And I invite you to come to the Soviet Union," said Gorbachev.

"I accept," said Ronald Reagan.

"I accept," said Gorbachev.

Gorbachev agreed to come to the United States in 1986.

Reagan agreed to go to Moscow in 1987.

*President Ronald Reagan (left) and Soviet leader Mikhail Gorbachev
approach each other for a handshake of greeting at the Villa Fleur
d'Eau at Versoix near Geneva on November 19, 1985. The first round of
summit talks was about to begin here.*

On the first day, Reagan and Gorbachev decided to change the script, which called for a formal conference. Instead, they talked one-on-one before a blazing fire and then walked together in the garden.

The first encounter between the two superpower leaders at the villa was cordial and relaxed.

The second day of the talks, with all the major participants sitting around a conference table at the Soviet mission in Geneva. They are (clockwise): United States Secretary of State George Shultz, President Reagan, White House Chief of Staff Donald Regan, United States Ambassador to Russia Arthur Hartman, Senior National Security staff member Jack F. Matlock, Soviet Ambassador to Washington Anatoly Dobrynin, Foreign Minister Eduard Shevardnadze, and Soviet leader Mikhail Gorbachev.

President Reagan and Gorbachev and their aides take an outdoor stroll between conferences.

The faces of leaders Reagan and Gorbachev seem to express a mood of amity and hope on both sides.

First Lady Nancy Reagan waves as she walks through the streets of St. Prex on Lake Geneva, accompanied by an admiring crowd of Swiss schoolchildren.

Smartly attired, Raisa Gorbacheva (right) and Nancy Reagan stand holding messages of hope for world peace, to be placed in the cornerstone of the new Red Cross Museum in Geneva. Earlier, at a luncheon of tea and cabbage pie, the press tried to raise an issue between the two ladies regarding their fashionable clothes as competition for attention with international affairs. Both handled the provocation adroitly, saying there were more important matters to discuss.

Speaking before the international press, the president offers his evaluation of the summit, while Premier Gorbachev, listening closely, waits his turn.

The president, at six feet one, seemed taller when he returned from Geneva. He had grown in his grasp of world problems. Before he left for Geneva, he had called the Soviet Union an "evil empire." He came back persuaded that the United States and the Soviet Union not only could but must do business with one another.

At seventy-five, late though it may be in life, Ronald Wilson Reagan achieved a new maturity in his view of the world. On his return, after his report to Congress on nationwide television, the polls showed that Reagan's public approval rating for handling foreign relations in general and the Soviets in particular had risen sharply to an astounding 81 percent.

Hope was expressed everywhere that the Geneva summit would finally lead to durable peace. Was it possible that the man known as "the Great Communicator" would earn a new sobriquet before he left office, "the Great Peacemaker"?

The DC-8 jet lifted off Gander Field in Newfoundland in a predawn mix of snow and freezing drizzle, carrying 248 young 101st Airborne soldiers on the last leg home from the Middle East to Fort Campbell, Kentucky.

Suddenly the plane faltered, dropped the thousand feet it had gained, and hit a small hill, exploding and disintegrating in flames that spread for a quarter of a mile. The eight crew

With a firm final handshake, President Reagan and Soviet leader Mikhail Gorbachev (left) conclude the summit meetings in the Geneva International Conference Center after issuing a joint statement. The historic talks did not solve the world's problems, but opened the way for better understanding between the superpowers and greater hope of peace.

President Reagan addresses a memorial service at Fort Campbell for the 248 101st Airborne soldiers who died tragically at Gander.

members and all 248 servicemen, coming home for Christmas after eighteen months in the Sinai desert on peace-keeping duties, died instantly, leaving a nation in shock.

Five days later, on December 17, 1985, the president, wearing a black suit, arrived with Nancy at Fort Campbell and entered Hangar 7 quietly and without ceremony to mourn the dead soldiers with their gathered families and friends.

There was a long silence as the president paused, then began to speak from the heart. "I know there are no words that can make your pain less. How I wish there were." He reminded them that all the young men were still with them. "Love lives on and sees us through sorrow. . . . From the moment love is born it is always with us, keeping us . . . strong in the time of trial. . . . In life they were our heroes, in death our loved ones, our darlings. . . . Love is never wasted, love is never lost. . . . Think for the moment of the joy you gave them and be glad. . . . They will never grow old; they will always be young."

When the service was over, the families rose to leave, but the president asked them to stay. He and Nancy came to them, speaking quietly with each family, one at a time, opening their arms and embracing these people as their neighbors. Many wept, filled with grief as they showed the president and First Lady pictures of lost sons and young husbands. Others were silent, beyond words. Some clung to the Reagans, who tried not to cry themselves. No one had ever seen a president so openly and deeply moved by tragedy and love.

Ronald Reagan with families of soldiers killed in the crash of a DC-8 in Canada, which was to bring them home for Christmas.

President Reagan and staff watch a television replay of the lift-off and tragic end of the space shuttle Challenger on January 28, 1986, in the president's White House study. In the first moments after Challenger lifted off from Launch Pad 39B at Cape Canaveral, Florida, all seemed to go well. Then came disaster, as the booster rockets exploded, carrying all seven men and women aboard the Challenger to a watery death.

The space ship *Challenger* thundered off the launch pad into the clear Florida sky, majestic in its magnificent technology—and then exploded before everyone's eyes, taking the lives of all seven astronauts and shaking the nation's faith in its ability to conquer space safely.

Four days later, on January 27, 1986, President Ronald Reagan joined the astronauts' families and friends in a memorial service at the Johnson Space Center in Houston. He had come not only to mourn but to transform a grieving country from pessimism to optimism.

"In this moment of shared loss," Ronald Reagan said, "the sacrifice of your loved ones has stirred the soul of our nation and, through the pain, our hearts have been opened to a profound truth. The future is not free, the story of all human progress is one of a struggle against all odds. . . .

President Reagan led the nation in mourning the lost heroes, shown above. Back row (left to right): Mission Specialist Eli Onizuka, Teacher in Space Participant Christa McAuliffe, Payload Specialist Greg Jarvis, and Mission Specialist Judith Resnick. Front row (left to right): Pilot Michael Smith, Commander Richard Scobee, and Mission Specialist Ronald McNair.

Pain registered on their faces, the astronauts' spouses and children join the president and First Lady at the memorial service at the Houston Space Center.

The president consoles Marcia Jarvis, widow of astronaut Gregory Jarvis, at the close of the memorial services. At her left are Claude, Lorna, and Janelle Onizuka—brother, wife, and daughter of lost astronaut Ellison Onizuka.

President Reagan and members of the Challenger families watch the dramatic flyover of air force fighter planes in a "missing man forma-tion," at a memorial service in Houston, Texas. Nancy Reagan stands behind and to the right of the president. There were better days to come for President Ronald Wilson Reagan and the nation.

"Dick, Mike, Judy, El, Ron, Greg, and Christa, your families and your country mourn your passing. We bid you good-bye. We will never forget you. For those who knew you well and loved you, the pain will be deep and enduring."

Ronald Reagan then reminded his audience that more teachers like Christa McAuliffe would journey into space as the United States continued to explore the far horizons. Evoking the spirit of the pioneer astronauts, he said, "They had that special grace that says, 'Give me a challenge and I'll meet it with joy.' The future doesn't belong to the fainthearted, it belongs to the brave. The *Challenger* crew was pulling us into the future, and we will continue to follow them." The president found meaning in the astronauts' death and offered hope in exchange for sorrow, a bright tomorrow rather than futility.

Recent polls have named Ronald Reagan as probably the most popular president of this century. It is most unusual for the American people to so admire a president, even when disagreeing with particular policies. When he ordered the invasion and liberation of Grenada, for example, he gave America back some sense of the inner strength and destiny that it lost in Vietnam. How can one not admire a man who says, "Under this administration our nation is through wringing its hands and apologizing"?

Ronald Reagan is the stuff of legend, surviving both attempted assassination and cancer. A third-generation Irish-American in a nation of immigrants, he is so completely rooted in small-town life and our nation's frontier spirit that he has become a uniquely American hero.

SELECTED BIBLIOGRAPHY

Adler, Bill. *Ronnie and Nancy: A Very Special Love Story.* New York: Crown, 1985.

_____. *The Reagan Wit.* Aurora, Illinois: Caroline House, 1981.

Boyarsky, Bill. *The Rise of Ronald Reagan.* New York: Random House, 1968.

_____. *Ronald Reagan: His Life and Rise to the Presidency.* New York: Random House, 1981.

Cannon, Lou. *Reagan.* New York: G. P. Putnam's Sons, 1982.

de Mause, Lloyd. *Reagan's America.* New York: Creative Roots, Inc., 1984.

Dugger, Ronnie. *On Reagan: The Man and His Presidency.* New York: McGraw-Hill, 1983.

Ford, Gerald R. *A Time to Heal: The Autobiography of Gerald R. Ford.* New York: Harper and Row, 1979.

Hannaford, Peter. *The Reagans: A Political Portrait.* New York: Coward-McCann, 1983.

Leamer, Laurence. *Make Believe: The Story of Nancy and Ronald Reagan.* New York: Harper and Row, 1983.

McClelland, Doug. *Hollywood on Ronald Reagan: Friends and Enemies Discuss Our President, the Actor.* Winchester: Faber and Faber, 1983.

Reagan, Nancy, and Bill Libby. *Nancy.* New York: William Morrow, 1980.

Reagan, Ronald, and Richard G. Hubler. *Where's the Rest Of Me?* New York: Duell, Sloan, and Pierce, 1965.

Reedy, George. *The Twilight of the Presidency.* New York: World Publishing Co., 1970.

Thomas, Tony. *Ronald Reagan: Hollywood Years.* Secaucus: Citadel Press, 1980.